Dartmouth College
Hanover, New Hampshire

Written by Scott L. Glabe
Edited by Janos D. Marton

Additional contributions by Omid Gohari,
Christina Koshzow, Chris Mason, Joey Rahimi,
Jon Skindzier, Luke Skurman, Tim Williams
and Kristen Burns

COLLEGE PROWLER

ISBN # 1-59658-038-0
ISSN# 1551-0323
© Copyright 2005 College Prowler
All Rights Reserved
Printed in the U.S.A.
www.collegeprowler.com

Special thanks to Babs Carryer, Andy Hannah, LaunchCyte, Tim O'Brien, Bob Sehlinger, Thomas Emerson, Andrew Skurman, Barbara Skurman, Bert Mann, Dave Lehman, Daniel Fayock, Chris Babyak,The Donald H. Jones Center for Entrepreneurship, Terry Slease, Jerry McGinnis, Bill Ecenberger, Idie McGinty, Kyle Russell, Jacque Zaremba, Larry Winderbaum, Paul Kelly, Roland Allen, Jon Reider, Team Evankovich, Julie Fenstermaker, Lauren Varacalli, Abu Noaman, Jason Putorti, Mark Exler, Daniel Steinmeyer, Jared Cohon, Gabriela Oates, Tri Ad Litho, David Koegler, and Glen Meakem.

Bounce Back Team: Michael Ellis, Nikhil Gore, Nicholas Schwartz

College Prowler™
5001 Baum Blvd.
Suite 456
Pittsburgh, PA 15213

Phone: (412) 697-1390, 1(800) 290-2682
Fax: (412) 697-1396, 1(800) 772-4972
E-mail: info@collegeprowler.com
Website: www.collegeprowler.com

Welcome to College Prowler™

During the writing of College Prowler's guidebooks, we felt it was critical that our content was unbiased and unaffiliated with any college or university. We think it's important that our readers get honest information and a realistic impression of the student opinions on any campus — that's why if any aspect of a particular school is terrible, we (unlike a campus brochure) intend to publish it. While we do keep an eye out for the occasional extremist — the cheerleader or the cynic — we take pride in letting the students tell it like it is. We strive to create a book that's as representative as possible of each particular campus. Our books cover both the good and the bad, and whether the survey responses point to recurring trends or a variation in opinion, these sentiments are directly and proportionally expressed through our guides.

College Prowler guidebooks are in the hands of students throughout the entire process of their creation. Because you can't make student-written guides without the students, we have students at each campus who help write, randomly survey their peers, edit, layout, and perform accuracy checks on every book that we publish. From the very beginning, student writers gather the most up-to-date stats, facts, and inside information on their colleges. They fill each section with student quotes and summarize the findings in editorial reviews. In addition, each school receives a collection of letter grades (A through F) that reflect student opinion and help to represent contentment, prominence, or satisfaction for each of our 20 specific categories. Just as in grade school, the higher the mark the more content, more prominent, or more satisfied the students are with the particular category.

Once a book is written, additional students serve as editors and check for accuracy even more extensively. Our bounce-back team — a group of randomly selected students who have no involvement with the project — are asked to read over the material in order to help ensure that the book accurately expresses every aspect of the university and its students. This same process is applied to the 200-plus schools College Prowler currently covers. Each book is the result of endless student contributions, hundreds of pages of research and writing, and countless hours of hard work. All of this has led to the creation of a student information network that stretches across the nation to every school that we cover. It's no easy accomplishment, but it's the reason that our guides are such a great resource.

When reading our books and looking at our grades, keep in mind that every college is different and that the students who make up each school are not uniform — as a result, it is important to assess schools on a case-by-case basis. Because it's impossible to summarize an entire school with a single number or description, each book provides a dialogue, not a decision, that's made up of 20 different topics and hundreds of student quotes. In the end, we hope that this guide will serve as a valuable tool in your college selection process. Enjoy!

OMID GOHARI ○ CHRISTINA KOSHZOW ○ CHRIS MASON ○ JOEY RAHIMI ○ LUKE SKURMAN ○
The College Prowler™ Team

Table of Contents

Introduction from the Author

To be perfectly honest, I had little intention of attending Dartmouth when I decided to ship off my Common Application to Hanover. However, December's afterthought became April's dream school as I started learning about the northernmost and most unique institution in the storied Ivy League. Today, I wouldn't trade my chance to attend Dartmouth for anything, for I've discovered that students are privy to the best undergraduate experience in the nation while attending the College on the Hill.

There are three reasons why I lavish such a superlative, the first being that—unlike so many other institutions these days—the College experience at Dartmouth is truly undergraduate. Professors teach every class and generally treat students like royalty. Sure, Dartmouth has a few graduate students, but they skitter about on the edge of campus, while everything important to undergrads surrounds the Green. Moreover, with a liberal arts focus and small campus size, Dartmouth truly is a college, a single college. In the absence of artificial barriers, academic or otherwise, a unified community is molded.

The strange creature known as the Dartmouth Plan provides another bonus unique to the College. A fabulous Sophomore Summer means an off-term somewhere else along the line, which leads to fantastic school-year internships. Most importantly, the flexibility engendered by all this switching about has birthed the best study abroad program in the country, allowing Dartmouth students to literally travel the world during their four years in school.

Most vital to the College is its school spirit. The wild parties that seemingly continue from Wednesday through Sunday of Homecoming, Winter Carnival, or Green Key Weekend are just a Dionysian manifestation of the jovial enthusiasm that endures all year long. Sometimes it seems as if the entire student body will jam into a single happening fraternity on any given night if only word of a party is disseminated. But more enduring than all that free-flowing is the reputation forged in New Hampshire granite, the reputation of a school where everyone works hard, plays hard, and exudes a rugged individualism. If the pocketbooks and fervor of alumni are to judge, such an experience is and will continue to be unattainable elsewhere, presuming the rather draconian administration knows when to stop tinkering.

You can get an education anywhere, and there are fantastic schools everywhere, especially on the East Coast. However, what drew me to Dartmouth and what sets it apart is the quality of life its students are afforded. There are lots of places that provide similar learning, but nowhere, I believe, is there better living than at the College on the Hill.

Scott L. Glabe, Author
Dartmouth Class

By the Numbers

General Information

Dartmouth College
Hanover, NH
03755

Control:
Private

Academic Calendar:
Quarter

Religious Affiliation:
None

Founded:
1769

Website:
http://www.dartmouth.edu

Main Phone:
(603) 646-1110

Admissions Phone:
(603) 646-2875

Student Body

Full-Time Undergraduates:
4,039

Part-Time Undergraduates:
59

Full-Time Male Undergraduates:
2,091

Full-Time Female Undergraduates:
2,007

Female:Male Ratio
49%:51%

Admissions

Overall Acceptance Rate:
18%

Total Applicants:
11,855

Total Acceptances:
2,155

Freshman Enrollment:
1,092

Yield (% of admitted students who actually enroll):
50.6%

Early Decision Available?
Yes

Early Action Available?
No

Total Early Decision Applicants:
1,114

Total Early Decision Acceptances:
33%

Early Decision Deadline:
November 1

Regular Decision Deadline:
January 1

Total Regular Decision Acceptances:
17%

Must-Reply-By Date:
May 1

Applicants Placed on Waiting List:
1,296

Applicants Accepted From Waiting List:
840

Students Enrolled From Waiting List:
54

Transfer Applications Received:
314

Transfer Students Accepted:
36

Transfer Students Enrolled:
22

Transfer Acceptance Rate:
61%

Common Application Accepted?
Required

Supplemental Forms?
Yes

Admissions Phone:
(603) 646-2875

Admissions E-mail:
admissions.office@dartmouth.edu

Admissions Website:
http://www.dartmouth.edu/admissions

SAT I or ACT Required?
Either

**SAT I Range
(25th – 75th Percentile):**
1330 – 1530

**SAT I Verbal Range
(25th – 75th Percentile):**
660-760

**SAT I Math Range
(25th – 75th Percentile):**
670-770

**First-Year Students
Submitting SAT Scores:**
89.5%

Retention Rate:
$96

**Top 10% of
High School Class:**
84%

Application Fee:
$65

Financial Information

Full-Time Tuition:
$30,465

Room and Board:
$9,000

Books and Supplies for class:
$2,386

**Average Need-Based
Financial Aid Package:**
$25,945
(including loans, work-study,
grants, and other sources)

**Students Who
Applied For Financial Aid:**
60%

Students Who Received Aid:
51%

Financial Aid Forms Deadline:
February 1

Financial Aid Phone:
(603) 646-2451

Financial Aid E-mail:
Financial.Aid@dartmouth.edu

Financial Aid Website:
http://www.dartmouth.edu/apply/financialaid

Academics

The Lowdown On...
Academics

Degrees Awarded:
Bachelor's, Postbachelor's certificate, Master's, Doctoral, First professional

Most Popular Areas of Study:
12% economics, 9% psychology, 8% history, 8% political science and government, 7% English language and literature

Undergraduate Schools:
College (students may also apply to Thayer School of Engineering)

Full-Time Faculty:
644

Faculty with Terminal Degree:
82.7%

Student-to-Faculty Ratio:
8.5: 1

Average Course Load:
Three

Four Year Graudation Rate:
86%

Five Year Graudation Rate:
93%

Six Year Graudation Rate:
95%

Special Degree Options
Combined bachelor's of arts and bachelor's of engineering

AP Test Score Requirements
Possible credit for scores of 3, 4, or 5

IB Test Score Requirements
Possible credit for scores of 6 or 7

Did You Know?
• Dartmouth ranks **#9** in U.S. News and World Report's latest edition of America's Best Colleges.

• According to the Institute of International Education, Dartmouth has the highest fraction of students who **study abroad** (47%).

• In need of luck during finals? Just rub the nose of **Warner Bentley's bust** in the Hopkins Center.

• A perennial powerhouse, the Dartmouth Forensic Union policy **debate team** has won six national championships.

• Dartmouth students measure their progress towards graduation with **credits** rather than hours; each class counts as one credit.

Sample Academic Clubs: College Bowl, Mock Trial Society, Forensic Union, Daniel Webster Legal Society, Club of Dartmouth Entrepreneurs

Best Places to Study
Novack Café, The Stacks, Baker Tower Room, the Collis Center, dorm lounge/study spaces.

Students Speak Out On...
Academics

"It's pretty easy to understand why Dartmouth is so alluring. The student body has top-notch academics available without any competition for resources from graduate students. With teaching-centered professors across the board, Dartmouth's academics are challenging, personal, and tailored for the intellectual development of individual students."

Q "As for academics, **they're amazing**. The professors are great; you get to talk to them a lot more than at other colleges of similar merit."

Q "Academics at Dartmouth are unbeatable. Since we aren't in the classroom very much compared to students at other schools, there is a lot of independent work, and it moves quickly. **If you like to be challenged** and move at a quickpace, you'll love Dartmouth."

Q "Dartmouth's true strength academically is its strong commitment to undergraduate education. **Classes are small** and professors are easy to approach, helpful, and caring about their students. Distribution requirements exist, but are not onerous—there are always classes available like the "Technology of Sailing" for humanities people to get rid of their science distributives.

Q **"There's room for improvement**—a core curriculum of Western civilization course would be far more enriching than half of the schlock from the women's and various ethnic studies departments."

Q "One nice thing is that, other than an English class that you can test out of and a freshman writing seminar, **there are no mandatory courses.** The distributive requirements are very general and give you a chance to take some really fun classes."

Q "While classes vary in difficulty, **it's not very hard to get a B+,** which is the campus-wide median. Go to class, do your reading, and you should do just fine."

Q **"Small classes are a huge plus.** Intro courses that might have a few hundred students elsewhere have fifty at Dartmouth. While some social science departments are bigger, most upper-level classes have enrollments of a couple dozen or so."

Q "**The teaching staff is incredible.** Profs are very accessible and usually very willing to help. I doubt you'll find profes sers so willing to meet with you individually anywhere else."

Q "The teachers are great, for the most part. **They're all easily approachable** through office hours, before or after class, and through BlitzMail, our e-mail system."

Q "Talk to upperclassmen to find out which professors to get. **Often it's the professor that makes the class worth anything,** not the subject material. Foreign study programs are also a good idea. But plan early! I ended up stuck in Mexico."

Q "Honestly, **there's not enough discourse in classes.** I've lost my ability to speak in groups from being out-of-practice in class. Some professors are wonderful and have become mentors and friends, but on the whole I'm disappointed by the academics. The history department is an exception—I've enjoyed 90% of the classes there. College Courses are a waste of time."

Q **"Study abroad**! The programs are easy to apply for and an awesome experience. There are three main types: foreign study, which anyone can apply for but are run by major departments; language study, which you can use to meet your language requirement; and exchange programs, which Dartmouth has with a bunch of other schools all over."

Q "With the D-plan, **you get one off term during the school year,** which helps you to land lots of sweet jobs and internships. However, be prepared not to see your friends for a year or more."

Q "The Student Assembly maintains **a website where students review classes they've taken** (http://sa.dartmouth.edu/guide). It's a great way to see whether a course you're interested in is good or bad."

Q **"Freshman advisors are usually worthless,** but you can wander into any department to get advice."

The College Prowler Take On...
Academics

Attending Dartmouth is a surefire way to avoid those troublesome TAs, as all classes are taught by professors. While there are some duds to be avoided, students consistently cite their profs as the most outstanding part of their academic experience. Professors are rarely sidetracked by research, and a low student-to-faculty ratio makes getting to know your instructors a breeze. Various study abroad programs are another student favorite, whether strolling the hallowed halls of Oxford or chasing sheep in New Zealand is more your cup of tea. The Dartmouth Plan facilitates taking a variety of exchange programs and terms abroad. With ten-week terms, students enjoy modest three-term course loads, and that pesky organic chemistry class will be over in no time. Sophomore Summer (sounds better than "summer school," right?) is a blast, but scattered off terms are hard on amorous and platonic relationships alike.

As would be expected of an institution of Dartmouth's caliber, classes are challenging, professors are brilliant, and academic experiences are positive in the vast majority of cases. "Work hard, play hard" is an apt motto. While Dartmouth students let loose on weekends and remain surprisingly uncompetitive when it comes to grades, most study more than they let on, particularly as finals draw near.

The College Prowler™ Grade on
Academics: A

A high Academics grade generally indicates that professors are knowledgeable, accessible, and genuinely interested in their students' welfare. Other determining factors include class size, how well professors communicate, and whether or not classes are engaging.

Local Atmosphere

The Lowdown On...
Local Atmosphere

Region:
Northeast

City, State:
Hanover, New Hampshire

Setting:
Small town

Distance from New York:
4.5 hours

Distance from Boston:
2.5 hours

Distance from Montreal:
2.5 hours

Points of Interest:
Quechee Gorge
Simon Pearce Glassblowing
and Restaurant
Ben and Jerry's Factory
New England Transportation
Museum
The Ledges

Closest
Shopping Malls:

West Lebanon Shopping Plaza

Closest
Movie Theatres:

The Nugget on Main Street
The Loew Auditorium in the
Hopkins Center

Major Sports Teams:

Boston Red Sox (baseball)
Boston Celtics (basketball)
Boston Bruins (hockey)
New England Patriots
(football)

City Websites
http://www.hanovernh.org

5 Fun Facts about Hanover:

1. Hanover is located in a scenic region known as the **Upper Valley,** which includes the scenic area in both New Hampshire and Vermont that borders the Connecticut River.

2. Eager for a hike? The **Appalachian Trail** runs right through town.

3. The **town charter** was granted in 1761 by King George III to settlers from Connecticut.

4. Hanover and Norwich, VT formed the first **interstate school district** in the United States.

5. Hanover was recently ranked the seventh **best college town** in the nation by Outside magazine.

Famous Hanoverian:

Bill Bryson- the author of "A Walk in the Woods". Some say J.D Salinger is cooped up right outside of Hanover, but no one can know for sure.

"Hanover is a very, very, very small New England town. We are literally in the middle of nowhere, although it's still easy to get to. It is right off of I-91N. It's a very beautiful campus; anyone who has been to Dartmouth will tell you that."

Q "The campus is pretty cool—really pretty and everything. **I like it because it's really peaceful.** You won't hear much about the rest of the world when you're up there except if you want to read the newspaper."

Q "The **town life revolves around the college.** This is one of the coolest things about Dartmouth—being immersed in an environment that is totally devoted to education. There isn't so much to see in the town, but there's enough stuff to do on campus to make up for that."

Q "Hanover is a quaint little college town. If you want to get a good feel of what the campus is like without visiting, imagine the stereotypical 'college' atmosphere—large grassy lawns, distinguished brick buildings, a feeling of knowledge and history. **Dartmouth is essentially the archetypical New England college,** nestled into the almost unbearably picturesque Connecticut River Valley."

Q "It's quaint. Very small. **We have everything we need and nothing else.** It's boring at times, but it's cute and I like it. It's very isolated though."

Q **"The atmosphere is gorgeous.** It's a small town feel combined with the college town atmosphere. I wouldn't want to go to school anywhere else. On the campus itself, there is an amazing sense of community that EVERYONE notices and raves about."

Q "Beautiful. **Take advantage of it, e**ven if it's to the detriment of your GPA. You'll most likely never get to experience this beauty again. I only wish it wasn't so cloudy so often."

Q "Not only is the area beautiful, but there is so much to do outside. **I hiked the Appalachian Trail for Freshman Trips,** rented a DOC cabin with friends for cheap, and skied at the Dartmouth Skiway, which is just fifteen minutes from campus. Also, taking the rope swing into the river is a must."

Q "There's no culture in Hanover, but, thankfully, Dartmouth brings culture to you. I think **there's an average of three artistic events a day on campus,** including a lot of movies. Best of all, everything's just five bucks for students."

Q "It's a rural campus with small towns around and no big places to go, so you stay on campus a lot. **People take road trips** to Boston and Montreal a lot."

Q "The town is very small but cute. **We're two hours from Boston,** the closest real city."

Q "Dartmouth's atmosphere blends New England architecture and history with Southern hospitality and West Coast relaxation to create the perfect environment for a successful and happy college career. The city of Hanover has a fruitful partnership with Dartmouth, and **the local atmosphere promotes friendly interpersonal interaction.** While Hanover doesn't have the hustle and bustle of the Big Apple, it does have a pervasive 'feel good' atmosphere that is infectious."

Q "As far as the campus goes, **it's in a pretty, small, upscale town.** It's really beautiful but certainly not a booming metropolis."

Q "There's really **nothing except for some restaurants and stores,** just scenic New England stuff and a very pretty campus. There's not really anything to stay away from either. Dartmouth is 'in the sticks,' which can be pleasant, but it can also suck."

Q "Hanover is **pretty dull** unless you're a big outdoorsy person, the local area won't be a big bonus. The school's atmosphere is quite nice and idyllic—it's hard even as a jaded/bitter senior to not think warmly of the campus."

Q "The Upper Valley's a beautiful place, and **there's fun places** in the area if you're willing to do a little exploring. Lots of people take day trips to Quechee or other small towns in New Hampshire and Vermont."

The College Prowler Take On...
Local Atmosphere

Hanover is unfailingly described as "small". However, with a full-service school like Dartmouth, who needs anything else? In fact, most Dartmouth students are so busy that they rarely ponder what's beyond Wheelock Street. Those who do are usually thrilled by their placid surroundings. Situated just across the Connecticut River from Vermont in the scenic Upper Valley, Hanover is consistently praised for its peaceful New England beauty. Unless you're satisfied donning apparel from The Gap, you'll have to hitch a ride to nearby West Lebanon or another of Hanover's less ritzy neighbors to find chain stores of any kind.

Hanover's isolation facilitates the insular community that is a Dartmouth hallmark. With nowhere to go and little to do, students form tight-knit bonds that foster a love for the "College on the hill." Given the long travel time to major cities, "the Dartmouth bubble" is difficult to burst, though road trips are common. While culture junkies should expect boredom, the rugged type will enjoy the region's unparalleled outdoor opportunities.

The College Prowler™ Grade on
Local
Atmosphere: C-

A high Local Atmosphere grade indicates that the area surrounding campus is safe and scenic. Other factors include nearby attractions, proximity to other schools, and the town's attitude toward students

Safety & Security

The Lowdown On...
Safety & Security

Number of Dartmouth Safety and Security Officers:
30

Police Phone:
(603) 646-2234

Safety Services:
Bicycle registrations, BlitzMail bulletins, Engraving of valuable items, Escort service, Rape Aggression Defense, Weapons storage

Health Services:
Appointments, pharmacy, X-rays, specialty clinics, fall vaccine, Counseling and Human Development department, women's health program, STD and HIV/AIDS testing, Sexual Assault Peer Advisors, Planned Parenthood

Health Center Office Hours
8 a.m-4 p.m , Seven days a week.

Did You Know?

• According to the FBI, Hanover is the **safest town** in New Hampshire, which is in turn the safest state in the U.S.

Students Speak Out On...
Safety & Security

"Security is excellent! I always feel safe."

"Dartmouth College is probably **one of the safest colleges you'll find anywhere**. Due to its location, there aren't exactly a lot of random sketchy people wandering about like you find on urban campuses. The College has installed security cards in all the residence halls. Personally, I think it is stupid and unnecessary, since I find the campus to be extremely safe. If it weren't for the Greek system, Safety and Security would likely have nothing to do at all. They mostly handle drunk frat boys."

"To be blunt, security is really not an issue. **They put locks on the front doors of our dorms,** and everybody thinks that it is a big joke. Virtually everyone leaves their doors unlocked all the time. College-sponsored Safety and Security officers patrol all the time and there are blue-light phones every twenty feet (at least it feels that way), but they're nearly always unneeded...I lost my key on the third day and never worried about [locking my door] again."

"Coming from the big city, **it was quite a shock to be able to stroll around campus at the wee hours of the morning with impunity.** Many people don't even lock the doors to their rooms. Neither myself nor anyone I know has ever felt threatened on campus, although the graveyard can be kind of spooky at night."

"I feel safer at Dartmouth than I feel anywhere else. I'm from a suburban town which is very safe, but Dartmouth is in a very, very, small community, and I never worry about anything happening there."

"I feel safer in Hanover than anywhere else. **There's almost no crime,** and the area is well-lighted."

"Dorm rooms are almost always left unlocked, and I have never met anyone at Dartmouth who has felt unsafe walking around campus."

"The worst that happens is that **people sometimes leave their bikes unlocked and they get 'borrowed,'** but they usually they turn up in a few days."

"We have **blue light emergency phones all over the place,** and Safety and Security officers patrol the campus. There is also an escort service at night. The biggest cases usually deal with keg confiscation, inebriates, and the occasional bike theft. The crime scene at Dartmouth is minimal."

"As for security and safety, don't worry. The biggest crime at Dartmouth is bike theft, and [perpetrators] usually return your bike when they're done with it. Dorms are always open; no one locks their doors. It's probably one of the safest campuses around, and even so, there is an awesome safety and security force that patrols and can help you out."

"The new blue-lighted kiosks and door locks (all dorm doors used to be unlocked 24/7) ostensibly provide **more security,** though most students didn't register the need for such things."

"The area is very safe; you just want to be sure to lock your door to make sure none of your stuff is stolen."

"You may have heard about the two professors who were murdered a couple of years back, but that happened at their home off campus. The Upper Valley and not just **Dartmouth is a very safe place generally"**

The College Prowler Take On...
Safety & Security

Because of Hanover's isolation and small size, most everyone on and around the campus is associated with Dartmouth. With no outside crime, occasional theft is virtually the only secure concern. Blue light safety phones are numerous in case you need a late-night escort or feel unsafe, and Safety and Security has a vigilant presence on campus just in case trouble arises.

With classes, activities, and friends to keep up with, college students shouldn't have to worry about personal safety. At Dartmouth, you don't have to. The campus evokes a simpler time as students freely stroll campus at all hours, most rooms are left unlocked, and all dorms can be accessed with your student ID.

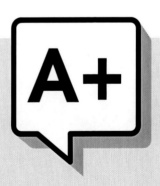

A+

The College Prowler™ Grade on

Safety & Security: A+

A high grade in Safety & Security means that students generally feel safe, campus police are visible, blue-light phones and escort services are readily available, and safety precautions are not overly necessary.

Computers

The Lowdown On...
Computers

High-Speed Network?
Yes

Wireless Network?
Yes

Number of Labs:
Four, plus departmental labs

Number of Computers:
100

Operating Systems:
Windows
Macintosh
UNIX

Free Software

Adobe Acrobat Reader, Adobe Photoshop, ArcView, BlitzMail, GreenPrint, Kerberos, QuickTime, Maple, Matlab, Mathematica, Netscape, SPSS 11, Stata 7

24-Hour Labs

Novack, in Berry Library.

Charge to Print?

Every student is allowed to print 600 pages for free each term, with exemptions given to thesis writers. After that, every page costs five cents.

Did You Know?

- The first school to have a **campus-wide wireless network,** Dartmouth was named the nation's "Most Wired" campus by Yahoo! in 1998.

Students Speak Out On...
Computers

"**Bringing your own computer is required, and for good reason. Blitzmail, our e-mail system, has basically taken over the role of the telephone for students. Everyone on campus uses it and students check it 'round the clock, practically. Laptops are increasingly popular because Dartmouth** has installed a wireless network so laptops can access the Internet from just about any building on campus."

Q "The network is as fast as those at most colleges. There's Ethernet, so **you can get up to about 1MB per second,** if you're transferring on campus."

Q "The computer access at Dartmouth is ridiculous. **I often wonder what we need so many computers and so much technology for.** We have every convenience and are spoiled rotten when it comes to this, so get excited!."

Q "Due to the fact that all undergrads need to have their own personal computers, **I just use my own.** The computer network, by and large, is fantastic. You can't beat Ethernet."

Q "You can't walk down a hallway without finding public **BlitzMail terminals that will soon dominate your life.** Plus, WiFi access everywhere means that with a laptop, the world is at your fingertips from the entire campus; doing research for a paper while sitting under a tree on the Green is not just an image plastered on brochures."

Q **"Everyone is required to purchase his own computer at Dartmouth.** You can buy from the school. There is a computer help facility called Kiewit inside the Berry Library."

Q "All students are required to have computers, which are connected to one of the fastest Internet Ethernet connections in the country. **There really aren't computer labs,** but there are public computers all over campus, so you never should have trouble finding one."

Q "The computer network is one of the best I've ever seen—everybody is required to have their own computer so **the labs aren't too big."**

Q **"All the labs are Mac,** but PCs are slowly coming around. Computer network is ultra fast, with good email client BlitzMail. There is a computer lab for non computer science people (around 40-50 good computers) as well as computers around campus in various places."

Q "Get a laptop. **Public computers are plentiful,** but it's nice to be able to listen to music in the library and not have to blitz files to yourself constantly."

Q "I'd say the student body is pretty **evenly split over PCs versus Macs.** Now that the school has started buying PCs for itself, it's uncertain whether Macs will decline in popularity."

Q "There are a handful 24-hour machines by Novack Café, but the College still lacks a central computer lab. First floor Berry is the biggest, but **it's literally impossible to get any work done** there with all the people traipsing through."

Q **"Definitely buy a computer from the school** rather than bring one. Computing Services will only provide support for models that the College sells."

Q "It's amazing **how dependent we are on e-mail.** I actually heard some older students laugh at a freshman who gave a guy her phone number. The Class of 2005 is the first to have cell phones in large numbers, and upperclassmen used to yell at you if you're using a phone in a public place."

Q "As one of the **most wired campuses in the country,** we have no shortage of computer access. Every student is required to have a computer, and there are computer terminals littered throughout campus. BlitzMail, the college e-mail system, is the dominant form of communication on campus, supplanting the use of the phone nearly entirely. The College has put BlitzMail terminals (computers solely devoted to 'blitzing') in basically every building. Laptops are extremely popular, and students frequently take advantage of the campus-wide wireless Internet by working on their laptops in a cafe, in a classroom, or lying on the Green."

Q "Many **younger students will use BlitzMail** and Instant Messenger."

Q "Our **public printing system is called GreenPrint.** It's really easy to install, and printers are located throughout campus. It was free, but the College is going to start charging because people use so much paper."

Q "Class registration is entirely electronic and takes about five minutes. **It's really easy to add, drop, or change classes.** The Banner Student website where you register also has your grades, allows to sign up for PE classes, and all sorts of other stuff."

The College Prowler Take On...
Computers

Dartmouth's campus-wide wireless network is incredibly convenient and widely acclaimed, providing Internet and email access to everywhere from dorm lounges to the Green. Just don't let your professor catch you following your hometown team during class! All dorm rooms and many public spaces are equipped with Ethernet ports. Computers are used most often for the ubiquitous BlitzMail, and the Dartmouth Name Directory makes it easy to e-mail everyone from professors to that girl in your history class. All freshmen are to bring or purchase have a computer, and most choose to buy one from the school for convenience.

Dartmouth students enter with their computers and use them obsessively, so much so that room phones are never used and cell phones are just beginning to have a presence on campus. Since the College just switched from Macs to PCs, computer labs now contain both Dell and Apple machines. Kiewit Computing Services, though uniformly unhelpful, provides support for both types of comps. While the labs are too small and overcrowded, Dartmouth's online registration and public printing systems are both very easy-to-use.

The College Prowler™ Grade on

Computers: A

A high grade in Computers designates that computer labs are available, the computer network is easily accessible, and the campus' computing technology is up-to-date.

Facilities

The Lowdown On...
Facilities

Student Center:
Collis

Athletic Center:
Alumni Gym, with the Kresge
Fitness Center located inside.

Libraries:
8

Popular Places to Chill:
Collis Commonground
The Green
Novack Café

Campus Size in Acres:
200

➡

What Is There to Do On Campus?

For quick fun, shoot some pool in the basement of Thayer Dining Hall or Collis Student Center. Not sweaty enough for you? Swim or lift weights at Alumni Gym for indoor exercise or explore the great outdoors with an afternoon of skiing or hiking. Go to a light night "AREA" student art exhibit, or watch one of the many a capella groups tear up a Greek house or random street corner.

Movie Theatre on Campus?

The Loew Auditorium.

Bowling on Campus?

No, but there is a hot bowling alley in White River Junction, 10 minutes away.

Bar on Campus?

Lone Pine Tavern.

Coffeehouse on Campus?

Big Green Bean.

Favorite Things to Do:

There's always an event going on at the Hopkins Center. Movies are popular, or you can rent your own from Jones Media Center in Berry Library. Students mob the Green when it's warm enough to be outside, particularly at the beginning of spring. Collis Commonground is home to everything from conferences to volunteer fairs to dance parties.

Did You Know?

• Sanborn Library serves **tea every weekday** at 4 p.m.

• Hopkins Center architect **Wallace Harrison** also designed the Lincoln Center and United Nations Building.

Students Speak Out On...
Facilities

{ **"Everything's very nice and new. I have almost no complaints, and anything I would want to change is probably being renovated within the next few years."**

Q "The **gym is really nice.** I work out often so I'm there a bunch. Squash courts, basketball, tennis, swimming, weight lifting, and a whole lot more."

Q "On the whole, **the infrastructure is a bit old,** if well-maintained. Most of the dorms date from the 1920's and have not been changed much since. But what is lost in modernity is made up for in charm."

Q **"Facilities are for the most part very good.** The gym is often criticized but beyond that, the facilities here are top notch. The great thing is that undergraduates have access to anything the College owns. If you want to do some research with the MRI Dartmouth owns, you don't need to wait 'til you're a med. school student. You can sign up to use it."

Q "I don't if this counts as facilities, but **the College has two land grants.** The Dartmouth Outing Club maintains hundreds of miles of trails, as well as a bunch of cabins all over New Hampshire. I guess the Skiway and the Connecticut River would be considered nice facilities, and you can rent the stuff you need for either."

Q "A lot of people don't like Berry Library, but I don't mind it. **There are plenty of places to study,** and be sure to check out the Tower Room when you visit. It's on the third floor of Baker and provides the most ideal Ivy League setting anywhere on campus."

Q "There are **plans to build an entire mini-campus north of the library,** which would add much-needed dorm space. However, given the current budget crisis, it may not be built for a while."

Q **"Novack Café is the most social place to be** on Sunday night or right before midterms. It's open till 2AM, and everyone goes there to procrastinate and hang out while their ostensibly studying."

Q "**Dorm lounges vary in quality.** The study space in East Wheelock is ridiculous, while the Choates basements are dungeons."

The College Prowler Take On...
Facilities

Students are generally satisfied but thrilled with Dartmouth's facilities. While Alumni Gym meets the needs of many, the cramped weight room, also known as Kresge Fitness Center, provides the perfect reason not to work out. The enormous Baker/Berry combined with satellite libraries provide plenty of study space, although many students despise the antiseptic look of Berry's interior. The modern-looking Hopkins Center, the central location for performing arts, includes the spacious Spaulding Auditorium, is adjacent to the Hood Museum, and even contains a dining hall.

Baker Tower is the most notable architectural feature of Dartmouth's aesthetically-pleasing campus, while the white buildings of Dartmouth Row date to the eighteenth century and almost make you want to don some colonial garb. Most structures are of a classy brick-and-stone structure and remain well-maintained on the inside despite their age. Newer buildings, such as the Rockefeller Center, generally fit in well, although the soon-to-be-destroyed "Shower Tower" is an albatross. While Dartmouth has poured millions into new buildings, including Berry and the new pschyology and history buildings, the College is in need of more dorm space. While Collis is passable as a student center with its dining options, TV room, and common space, Dartmouth lacks a true central gathering place for students once the Green is overcome by snow.

B

The College Prowler™ Grade on

Facilities: B

A high Facilities grade indicates that the campus is aesthetically pleasing and well-maintained; facilities are state-of-the-art, and libraries are exceptional. Other determining factors include the quality of both athletic and student centers and an abundance of things to do on campus.

Campus Dining

The Lowdown On...
Campus Dining

Freshman Meal Plan Requirement?
Yes

Meal Plan Average Cost:
$2400 per year

Off-Campus Places to Use Your Meal Plan
None

24-Hour On-Campus Eating?
No

Places to Grab a Bite with Your Meal Plan

Collis Café
Location: Collis Student Center
Food: Various
Favorite Dish: Custom Omelet, Chicken Stir Fry with Peanut Sauce
Hours: Monday-Friday, 7 a.m.-7 p.m.

Courtyard Café
Location: Hopkins Center
Food: Greasy American
Favorite Dish: French Fries
Hours: Monday-Friday, 7 a.m.-7 p.m.

Food Court
Location: Thayer Dining Hall
Food: Various/American
Favorite Dish: Ranch Chicken Sandwich
Hours: Monday-Sunday, 11 a.m- 3 p.m and 5 p.m.- 1 a.m.

Homeplate
Location: Thayer Dining Hall
Food: Healthy
Favorite Dish: Sunday Breakfast Buffet
Hours: Monday-Friday, 11:45 a.m.- 2:30 p.m., 4:45 p.m.- 7p.m.; Saturday-Sunday, 6:45 a.m.- 9:45 a.m.

Lone Pine Tavern
Location: Collis Student Center
Favorite Dish: Mushroom Chardonnay Chicken
Hours: Monday- Sunday, 6 p.m.- 1 a.m.

Novack Café
Location: Berry Library
Food: Snack
Favorite Dish: Chocolate Chip Cookies
Hours: Monday-Friday, 6 a.m.- 2 a.m.

The Pavilion
Location: Thayer Dining Hall
Food: Kosher/Halal/Sakuhara
Favorite Dish: Cheese Bread
Hours: Monday-Friday, 11 a.m.- 9 p.m.

Student Favorites

Food Court, Collis, Courtyard Cafe

Other Options:

Grab a snack from Brace Commons in East Wheelock or from Topside Convenience Store in Thayer. While in Thayer, stop by The Blend for delicious specialty smoothies. Eager to eat on the run? Try Colonel Bogey's at Hanover Country Club or the Skiway Café on the slopes. Students can also spend their DA$H discretionary accounts at Café North or Byrne Hall, which primarily serve graduate students.

Did You Know?

• The Pavilion serves **kosher-for-Passover** meals during the Jewish holiday.

Students Speak Out On...
Campus Dining

"The food on campus is really good. They have anything from healthier food and stir fry to buffet style. There's the Hopkins Center, where most of the artsy people eat, since it's in the art building. There's also the main Food Court, and Homeplate, a healthier version of the regular stuff. There are a ton of options, and the food is really good. There's also a convenience store on campus where you can buy food with your meal card."

"**The food is so good!** There is always something good to eat."

"The food here is actually really good. I'm a fairly picky eater (and a vegetarian), and **I have never had trouble eating on campus.** The DBA system is far better than any meal plan system."

"The food is one of the best aspects of being a college student at Dartmouth. Inside Thayer dining hall alone, there are tons of options, including a grill/sandwich bar area, an exquisite kosher dining section, an upscale specialized-entree section, a smoothie and juice bar, and a small College-owned convenience store. **Food Court is the most popular dining option for students,** generally focusing American food, like cheeseburgers (and they are delicious burgers at that). The smoothie bar, the Blend, is also a tremendously popular option. Best of all, you can charge all food to your student card without having to worry about how many meals you have available."

Q "Yes, I know, the Ranch Chicken at Food Court gets kind of tired after a long winter term, but **the food here is certainly among the best** of its peers. Also, the declining balance accounts allow students to eat meals at any time—convenient, even if the food is overpriced."

Q "Aside from the fact that **the food is overpriced,** Dartmouth dining services offer more variety and higher quality food than most colleges do. I've been happy so far, anyway."

Q "The food is actually pretty good. We have one of the top-rated dining services in the nation. **Homeplate has a lot of health food,** Food Court is the main hall that's open really late, Westside is a buffet, the Courtyard Cafe has a grill line and to-go stuff, and Collis serves stir-fry and smoothies but has limited hours. That's pretty much the lowdown."

Q "The Thayer Food Court is excellent with **a big salad bar and pizza** among other dishes. There are also plenty of good places just off-campus."

Q **"The food is pretty damn good for a college.** Everyone pretty much eats at the dining halls. In town, there are great restaurants and pizza places that deliver till 2a.m."

Q **"Dartmouth is awesome, as far as food goes!** The food is honestly really good. Homeplate is probably my favorite. They have a great grill and sandwich bar and always have awesome hot meals and other stuff. There are a lot of good dining halls, though, not just that one. The food is pretty expensive but you just subtract money from your meal card, so you can eat whatever you want whenever you want, and you don't need cash. There are no set meal times or anything so you can just go grab some food whenever and subtract the price from your meal plan. It's a pretty cool system."

Q "There's an abundance of greasy/fried food if that's your thing. **Dining Services also does a good job of providing healthy meals** (especially at the always-trendy Collis). What we seem to lack is the more 'normal' food. The new kosher dining facility is great, though—never any lines and food of outstanding quality."

Q "You're forced to get a meal plan by the college, **so you just have a card to eat at the various dining halls,** and they subtract it from you account. It's kind of a rip-off, unless you shop smart. There is also a Dartmouth convenience store where you may also spend your meal plan dollars, but the prices are pretty high there."

Q "Food on campus is pretty good. **There is a lot of variety.** I went to get a sandwich at Food Court around midnight once, and right behind me in line was Ben Stein, from Ferris Bueller and Win Ben Stein's Money. It's not always that cool, but it was fun."

Q "There are some good non-Dartmouth restaurants around, but the campus dining service food can be mediocre. Some of it is real good, but it gets old after a while. **You can eat whenever you want,** so you can usually find a time when the places aren't crowded. If you want good food, though, you probably have to drive off-campus."

Q "Good compared to other schools, but the healthy options are often overpriced. Go to the supermarket and cook for yourself and you'll save money. Contrary to popular opinion, **it takes less time to cook your own meal than to go to a dining hall,** wait in line for your food, to pay, and to eat in a crowded cafeteria where you'll get into conversations with five people you know."

The College Prowler Take On...
Campus Dining

Dartmouth is that rare school where students speak fondly about their campus food. While all the selections in the cafeteria are certain to get old, sumptuous options like the nutritious Home Plate or the greasy Courtyard Café will almost make you forget about mama's secret-recipe lasagna.

Variety and flexibility are the name of the game. Students can eat at any establishment on campus. With no set meals times, they can do so whenever they want. Moreover, students can spend they're declining balance account however they wish, meaning no meals are lost once you stop waking up for breakfast. The food is expensive, and each item must be purchased individually, but savvy students know how to stretch their DBA.

The College Prowler™ Grade on
Campus Dining: B

Our grade on Campus Dining addresses the quality of both school-owned dining halls and independent on-campus restaurants as well as the price, availability, and variety of food.

Off-Campus Dining

The Lowdown On...
Off-Campus Dining

Restaurant Prowler:
Popular Places to Eat!

Applebee's
Food: American
Address: 280 Plainfield Road, West Lebanon
Phone: (603) 298-8608
Price: Cheap-Moderate

C & A Pizza
Food: Pizza
Address: 17 Lebanon Street, Hanover
Phone: (603) 643-2966
Price: Moderate

Cafe Buon Gustaio
Food: Italian
Address: 72 S Main St, Hanover
Phone: (603) 643-5711
Price: Expensive

→

Canoe Club
Food: American
Address: 27 Main St, Hanover
Phone: (603) 643-9660
Price: Moderate

Chili's
Food: American
Address: 200 South Main
Street, West Lebanon
Phone: (603) 298-0335
Price: Cheap-Moderate

China Lantern Buffet
Food: Chinese
Address: 267 Plainfield Road,
West Lebanon
Phone: (603) 298-8818
Price: Cheap-Moderate

Dirt Cowboy Cafe
Food: Coffee, etc.
Address: 9 South Main Street
Phone: (603) 643-1323
Price: Moderate

Everything But Anchovies
Food: Pizza
Address: 5 Allen, Hanover
Phone: (603) 643-6135
Price: Cheap

Fort Lou's
Food: Breakfast
Address: 151 Heater Road,
Lebanon
Phone: (603) 448-5512
Price: Cheap

Hanover Inn (Daniel Webster Room and Zin's Winebistro)
Food: American
2 S. Main, Hanover
Phone (603) 643-4300
Price: Expensive

India Queen
Food: Indian
Address: 44 South Main Street,
Hanover
Phone: (603) 643-6900
Price: Cheap

Jesse's Restaurant & Tavern
Food: Steak and Seafood
Address: Lebanon Road,
Hanover, NH 03755
Phone: (603) 643-4111
Price: Moderate

Jewel of India
Food: Indian
Address: 27 Lebanon Street,
Hanover
Phone: (603) 643-2217
Price: Moderate

Lou's Restaurant
Food: Breakfast
Address: 30 S Main Street,
Hanover
Phone: (603) 643-3321
Price: Cheap

Mai Thai Cuisine
Food: Thai
Address: 44 South Main
Phone: (603) 643-9980
Price: Moderate

Molly's Restaurant & Bar
Food: American
Address: 43 South Main Street, Hanover
Phone: (603) 643-2570
Price: Moderate

Panda House
Food: Chinese
Address: 3 Lebanon Street, Hanover
Phone: (603) 643-1290
Price: Cheap-Moderate

Ramunto's
Food: Pizza
Address: 68 South Main Street, Hanover
Phone: (603) 643-9500
Price: Moderate

Rosey's
Food: Coffee and Tea
Address: 15 Lebanon Street, Hanover
Phone: (603) 643-5282
Price: Cheap

Seven Barrel
Food: British
Address: Colonial Plaza, West Lebanon
Phone: (603) 298-5566
Price: Moderate

Subway (and Ben and Jerry's)
Food: Sanwiches (and Ice Cream)
Address: 11 Lebanon, Hanover
Phone: (603) 643-0360
Price: Cheap

Three Tomatoes
Food: Italian
Address: 1 Court Street, Lebanon
Phone: (603) 448-1711
Price: Moderate

Best Pizza:
Ramunto's

Best Chinese:
Panda House

Best Breakfast:
Lou's Restaurant

Best Place to Take Your Parents
Hanover Inn

Closest Grocery Store
Dartmouth Co-op on Lebanon Street

Did You Know?

24-Hour Eating
Fort Lou's in Lebanon, Food Stop on Main Street

Fun Facts
• Looking to stay up all night? Head to Fort Lou's. Watch area truckers start their day with a **fantastic breakfast** as you prepare to go to bed.

• Subway, Ben Jerry's and Starbuck's are the **only chain establishments** in Hanover.

Student Favorites
EBAs, Ramunto's, Dirt Cowboy, Murphy's, Molly's

Students Speak Out On...
Off-Campus Dining

"There are a couple Chinese or Thai places in town, as well as a couple nicer, non-specialty restaurants like Murphy's on the Green (overpriced because it looks British) and Molly's. There's also Lou's Diner, which isn't great, but it's cheap."

Q "Restaurants around here aren't bad. The campus runs right into Main Street and there are a few good ones there. Molly's is my personal favorite, but Murphy's and 5 Olde Nugget are good too."

Q "In town, there are great restaurants, and **EBAs pizza delivers until 2 a.m.** It may not be great pizza, but at two in the morning, who cares?"

Q "**This is fairly limited,** but considering Hanover's a small town in New Hampshire we're not doing too badly. Pretty much any type of food can be found, and everything's open really late."

Q "If you have a car **you can drive to West Lebanon,** where there's a McDonald's, a Burger King, and some good non-fast-food options. Without a car you still have access to Subway, Ben and Jerry's, and a number of decent sit-down places. Most of them aren't usually that crowded. There's some great pizza places too, but if you're from Chicago or New York City you probably won't agree."

Q **"No more expensive than what you'd spend on a dining hall meal,** and, contrary to popular opinion, you are indeed spending real money at the dining halls. Hanover offers some nice off campus places, such as Five Olde and Murphy's. Molly's is overrated but the bread is fabulous."

Q "If you want good Italian food, go to Three Tomatoes in Lebanon, and for Chinese food drive to Peking Tokyo, also in Leb. It's worth the drive. (Panda House is awful, and its health code policies are questionable). **The Co-Op is a great supermarket,** but Price Chopper in West Leb is much less expensive and with more options."

Q "There's a good Asian place right off-campus. **At Hanover restaurants, you pay in cash, or a use BB One,** which is like a debit account for food. I don't think it's affiliated with the College and it's only accepted by certain participating places."

Q **"Severely limited for those without a car.** Restaurants in Hanover are generally mediocre and expensive. Only Murphy's On the Green is really worth it. I'm salivating over their sweet potato fries as I write."

Q "This is one of the **weaker aspects of Dartmouth life,** although thankfully the on-campus dining makes up for the shortcomings of off-campus dining. Ethnic food offerings are limited: there is one Japanese food option (Bamboo Garden), one Chinese food option (Panda House), two Indian food options (India Queen and Jewel of India), and a few other nearby restaurants, including an Italian restaurant in West Lebanon."

Q "For upscale dining off-campus, Zin's Winebistro and the Hanover Inn provide high-quality classic fare, like prime rib, lamb, etc. The most notable restaurant in the area is Lou's Diner. **Lou's has been serving Dartmouth students for over fifty years,** and has perfected the art of huge portions and delicious food. Some students stay up until Lou's opens at 6:00 AM and get an early breakfast."

Q **"Restaurant quality varies.** There's one Thai restaurant that isn't particularly good and one Chinese place that is awful. Don't misunderstand; by 'one' I mean that they are literally the only Thai restaurant and only Chinese food in Hanover. Still, we have two very good pizza joints: Everything But Anchovies (EBAs) and Ramunto's."

Q "Molly's Restaurant or Murphy's On the Green are two notable restaurants on Main Street, if you don't feel like fast food. **Café Buon Gustaio is out of most student's price range** for the average meal but it's a great place to take a date—it is an excellent Italian restaurant that serves great, fresh food."

Q **"A Chili's just opened up in West Leb.** It's really good and about the only chain sit-down place around. West Leb also has a couple Chinese buffets, which are extremely greasy but good in their own way."

The College Prowler Take On...
Off-Campus Dining

While the campus food is good enough to keep students eating in the dining halls most of the time, one can only eat so many Food Court Double Burger Deals. When you finally venture off campus to sate your appetite, you'll find a surprisingly large selection of establishments for a town as small as Hanover. Everyone has their favorite restaurants and some they despise, but there's always somewhere to take your parents or that date, should you be so lucky.

With a few pizza places, a breakfast joint, and token ethnic establishments, Hanover has the essential eats—and nothing more. You can find even African food in the area, but, if the local Chinese or Thai restaurant doesn't sit well with you, you're out of luck to find another one. Turn to nearby West Leb for fast food or other chains, but such trips are usually well-planned excursions rather than everyday experiences. Hanover doesn't have any truly genuine eating experiences, and even the ethnic offerings smack of suburbia. However, the area provides sufficient sustenance for students making the occasional escape from the dining halls.

The College Prowler™ Grade on
Off-Campus Dining: C-

A high off-campus dining grade implies that off-campus restaurants are affordable, accessible, and worth visiting. Other factors include the variety of cuisine and the availability of alternative options (vegetarian, vegan, Kosher, etc.).

Campus Housing

The Lowdown On...
Campus Housing

Room Types:
One-room singles; one-, two-, and three-room doubles, two- and three-room triples, and three-room quads.

Best Dorms:
Gold Coast
East Wheelock
Mass Row

Worst Dorms:
River
Choates
The Lodge
Tree Houses

Large Dormitory Residences

Cluster: Butterfield-Russell Sage
Dorm: Butterfield
Floors: 3
Total Occupancy: 55
Co-Ed: Yes
Class Arrangement: Upperclass
Room Types: One-room singles, one-room doubles, two-room triples
Special Features: Substance-free

➡

Cluster: Butterfield-Russell
Sage
Dorm: Russell Sage
Floors: 4
Total Occupancy: 119
Co-Ed: Yes
Class Arrangement: Mostly
freshmen
Room Types: Mostly two-room
triples
Special Features: Substance-
free

Cluster: Gold Coast
Dorm: Gile
Floors: 4
Total Occupancy: 112
Co-Ed: By floor
Class Arrangement: Mixed
class
Room Types: One-room
singles, two- and three- room
doubles, three-room triples
Special Features: Half bath in
some rooms, non-smoking

Cluster: Gold Coast
Dorm: Lord
Floors: 4
Total Occupancy: 78
Co-Ed: By floor
Class Arrangement: Mixed
class
Room Types: One-room
singles, two- and three- room
doubles, three-room triples
Special Features: Half bath in
some rooms

Cluster: Gold Coast
Dorm: Streeter
Floors: 4
Total Occupancy: 67
Co-Ed: By floor
Class Arrangement: Mixed
class
Room Types: One-room
singles, two- and three- room

Streeter (*Continued...*)
doubles, three-room triples
Special Features: Half bath in
some rooms

Cluster: Choates/North
Dorm: Bissell
Floors: 3
Total Occupancy: 74
Co-Ed: By suite
Class Arrangement: All
freshmen
Room Types: One-room singles
and doubles combined into
eight-person suites
Special Features: Full bath for
each suite, adjoining lounge

Cluster: Choates/North
Dorm: Brown
Floors: 3C
Total Occupancy: 74
Co-Ed: By suite
Class Arrangement: All
freshmen
Room Types: One-room singles
and doubles combined into
eight-person suites
Special Features: Full bath for
each suite, adjoining lounge

Cluster: Choates/North
Dorm: Cohen
Floors: 3
Total Occupancy: 74
Co-Ed: By suite
Class Arrangement: All
freshmen
Room Types: One-room singles
and doubles combined into
eight-person suites
Special Features: Full bath for
each suite, adjoining lounge

Cluster: Choates/North
Dorm: Little
Floors: 3
Total Occupancy: 72
Co-Ed: By suite
Class Arrangement: All freshmen
Room Types: One-room singles and doubles combined into eight-person suites
Special Features: Full bath

Cluster: Choates/North
Dorm: North
Floors: 3
Total Occupancy: 72
Co-Ed: Yes
Class Arrangement: Upperclass
Room Types: One-room singles
Special Features: Quiet dorm

Cluster: East Wheelock
Dorm: Andres
Floors: 4
Total Occupancy: 82
Co-Ed: Yes
Class Arrangement: Mixed-class
Room Types: Suite-style, with students in singles or doubles sharing living area and full bath
Special Features: Residential community, Brace Commons, smoke-free

Cluster: East Wheelock
Dorm: McCulloch
Floors: 4
Total Occupancy: 80
Co-Ed: Yes
Class Arrangement: Mixed-class
Room Types: Suite-style, with students in singles or doubles sharing living area and full bath
Special Features: Brace Commons, smoke-free

Cluster: East Wheelock
Dorm: Morton
Floors: 4
Total Occupancy: 68
Co-Ed: Yes
Class Arrangement: Mixed-class
Room Types: Suite-style, with students in singles or doubles sharing living area and full bath
Special Features: Brace Commons, smoke-free

Cluster: East Wheelock
Dorm: Zimmerman
Floors: 4
Total Occupancy: 84
Co-Ed: Yes
Class Arrangement: Mixed-class
Room Types: Suite-style, with students in singles or doubles
Special Features: Brace Commons, smoke-free

Cluster: Fayers
Dorm: Mid Fayerweather
Floors: 4
Total Occupancy: 107
Co-Ed: Yes
Class Arrangement: Mixed-class
Room Types: Mostly two-room triples
Special Features: Smoke-free, half-bath in many rooms

Cluster: Fayers
Dorm: North Fayerweather
Floors: 4
Total Occupancy: 56
Co-Ed: Yes
Class Arrangement: Mixed-class
Room Types: Mostly two-room triples
Special Features: Smoke-free, half-bath in many rooms

Cluster: Fayers
Dorm: South Fayerweather
Floors: 4
Total Occupancy: 63
Co-Ed: Yes
Class Arrangement: Mixed-class
Room Types: Mostly two-room triples
Special Features: Smoke-free, half-bath in many rooms

Cluster: Rip-Wood-Smith
Dorm: Ripley
Floors: 3
Total Occupancy: 45
Co-Ed: Yes
Class Arrangement: Mixed-class
Room Types: Mostly singles, some one- and two-room doubles
Special Features: Smoke-free

Cluster: Rip-Wood-Smith
Dorm: Smith
Floors: 3
Total Occupancy: 47
Co-Ed: Yes
Class Arrangement: Mixed-class
Room Types: Mostly singles, some one- and two-room doubles
Special Features: Smoke-free

Cluster: Rip-Wood-Smith
Dorm: Woodward
Floors: 3
Total Occupancy: 45
Co-Ed: Yes
Class Arrangement: Mixed-class
Room Types: Mostly singles, some one- and two-room doubles
Special Features: Smoke-free

Cluster: Topliff/New Hamp and the Lodge
Dorm: The Lodge
Floors: 3
Total Occupancy: 72
Co-Ed: Yes
Class Arrangement: Upperclass
Room Types: One-room doubles
Special Features: Private baths

Cluster: Topliff/New Hamp and the Lodge
Dorm: New Hampshire
Floors: 4
Total Occupancy: 121
Co-Ed: Yes
Class Arrangement: Mixed-class
Room Types: Singles, doubles, triples, and quads
Special Features: None

Cluster: Topliff/New Hamp and the Lodge
Dorm: Topliff
Floors: 4
Total Occupancy: 174
Co-Ed: Yes
Class Arrangement: Upperclass
Room Types: Mostly singles
Special Features: Many rooms carpeted

Cluster: Mass Row and Hitchcock
Dorm: Hitchcock
Floors: 4
Total Occupancy: 111
Co-Ed: Yes
Class Arrangement: Mixed-class
Room Types: Singles, two-room doubles, and two- and three-room triples.
Special Features: Smoke free, half baths in some triples

Cluster: Mass Row and Hitchcock
Dorm: Mid Massachusetts
Floors: 4
Total Occupancy: 111
Co-Ed: Yes
Class Arrangement: Upperclass
Room Types: One-room doubles and two-room triples
Special Features: Private bath and shower, smoke free

Cluster: Mass Row and Hitchcock
Dorm: North Massachusetts
Floors: 4
Total Occupancy: 68
Co-Ed: Yes
Class Arrangement: Upperclass
Room Types: Singles, doubles, and two-room triples
Special Features: Private bath and shower, carpeted, smoke free

Cluster: Mass Row and Hitchcock
Dorm: South Massachusetts
Floors: 4
Total Occupancy: 68
Co-Ed: Yes
Class Arrangement: Upperclass
Room Types: Singles, doubles, and two-room triples
Special Features: Private bath and shower, carpeted

Cluster: River
Dorm: French
Floors: 3
Total Occupancy: 98
Co-Ed: Yes
Class Arrangement: All freshmen
Room Types: Singles, two- and three-room doubles
Special Features: Substance free, lounge, study rooms

Cluster: River
Dorm: Hinman
Floors: 3
Total Occupancy: 101
Co-Ed: Yes
Class Arrangement: All freshmen
Room Types: Singles, two- and three-room doubles
Special Features: Substance free, lounge, study rooms, snack preparation areas

Cluster: River
Dorm: McLane
Floors: 3
Total Occupancy: 87
Co-Ed: Yes
Class Arrangement: All freshmen
Room Types: Singles, two- and three-room doubles
Special Features: Lounge, study rooms, snack preparation areas

Cluster: River
Dorm: Tree Houses (Birch, Elm, Maple, Oak, Pine, Spruce)
Floors: 2
Total Occupancy: 84
Co-Ed: By floor
Class Arrangement: Upperclass
Room Types: One-room doubles
Special Features: Lounge, bathroom

Cluster: Wheeler/Richardson
Dorm: Wheeler
Floors: 4
Occupancy: 106
Co-Ed: Yes
Class Arrangement: Mixed-class
Room Types: Mostly doubles
Special Features: Half-bath

Cluster: Wheeler/Richardson
Dorm: Richardson
Floors: 4
Occupancy: 68
Co-Ed: By Floor
Class Arrangement: Mixed-class
Room Types: Mostly two-room doubles and triples
Special Features: None

Undergrads on Campus:

2,825 (70%-80%)

Number of Dormitories:

32 (plus 6 Treehouses)

Percentage of Students in Singles: 52%

Percentage of Students in Doubles: 32%

Percentage of Students inTriples/Suites: 11%

Percentage of Students in Apartments: 2%

Bed Type
Extra-long twin (39" x 80")

Not permitted:
Microwaves, pets

Cleaning Service?
In public areas. Cleaning of rooms available only in East Wheelock

What You Get
Bed, desk, chair, bookshelf, dresser, closet, Ethernet port, cable jack.

Also Available:
Affinity housing: French and Italian (in East Wheelock), Asian Studies Center, Shabazz Center for Intellectual Inquiry (home of Afro-American Society), Foley Cooperative, International House, La Casa, Latin American/Latino/Caribbean House, Native American House, smoke-free dorm arrangements, substance-free dorm arrangements.

Did You Know?
• All Dartmouth students receive **free cable,** and, as of last year, free long-distance calls.

Students Speak Out On...
Campus Housing

"I like the Gold Coast and Mass Row. The River is the farthest away from campus (about a 10 minute walk) but that's about it. The Choates aren't that great, but I think the dorms are generally nice. A lot of them have extra amenities (bathrooms, carpeting, fireplaces, etc.)."

Q "Try to **avoid the River and the Choates.** Everything else is really, really nice. Compared to other colleges, Dartmouth's dorms are like luxury hotel rooms!."

Q "You don't want to live in the River or the Choates. (Even those are bearable, though.) All other **dorms are really nice.** There are singles, doubles, triples, and quads. East Wheelock is ridiculously huge and posh."

Q "The dorms are for the most part really nice, but some really suck—stay away from the river dorms, and the Choates. Otherwise, they're pretty sweet. Some have big rooms. **I had a fireplace last year** and personal bathrooms are common."

Q "In terms of housing, the dorms are really nice. Most of them are old buildings with a lot of character. Some even have working fireplaces in the rooms. I lived in Wheeler last year in a small, one-room double with a fireplace. **My room was probably the smallest out of all my friends',** but it was in a great location. A lot of the rooms have two rooms for three people so you can have a sleeping room and a common room."

Q **"Housing is amazing.** I have had incredible rooms and rooming situations. I also think that Residential Life works really hard to make living on campus a great experience, and it is. Most people choose to live on campus because it's a great deal."

Q "Freshmen get assigned rooms but after that, there is a lottery where priority goes to the highest class. The school says **they always house everyone who wants on-campus housing** and that even though housing isn't officially guaranteed it always works out. I was kind of skeptical when I got waitlisted and basically freaked out but it ended up working out better than I planned. I have a single and the two girls I was going to room with are on the same floor in a double. I guess it is a pretty good system."

Q "Dorms really vary. **East Wheelock is the nicest dorm cluster on campus**; it's really like a three- or four-star hotel. The Choates, on the other hand, suck. They are an architectural nightmare, plain and simple, they are just ugly as all hell. The River is even worse-it's ugly and in the back of beyond. It is located behind the business and engineering schools, away from anything of use."

Q "I lived in the Choates freshman year. My room was small, and **I had an awesome floor** and loved being with all freshman."

Q **"Apply to East Wheelock as a freshman by all means.** Although the dorms are more administration-friendly (translation: full of feel-good programming to cater to every racial and ethnic minority, as well as a good deal of social engineering), the plush and spacious rooms with private baths are well worth it. Elsewhere, housing is a mixed bag—generally dismal for freshman and miserable for sophomores (the Treehouses are particularly bad) but ranges from good to outstanding for juniors and seniors."

Q "People talk a lot about how nice East Wheelock is or how bad the Choates and River are, but all the others dorms are really great. **By the time you're a junior, you more or less have your pick of rooms.**"

Q "Decent. Living in a fraternity or sorority house is great; go Greek if only to live in a house with friends. **Privately-owned houses are better than College-owned houses,** which often feel like single-sex dorms with their policies about moving in and out at certain times. Dorms have no homey feeling at all, though they can be spacious and pleasant. Having lived in East Wheelock, I appreciate the newer buildings, but living on West Campus is more convenient, unless you live at the gym."

Q **"Big rooms, great locations; what more could a college student want?** Dartmouth employs the cluster system, typically putting three or four dormitories together in a group. These clusters often form individual identities, and students generally associate themselves as being from the Choates, The River, Mass Row, etc, as opposed to their individual dorms. Since Dartmouth is organized around the Green, all dorms are within easy walking distance of each other. That means there really aren't any poorly located dorms.

Q "While the sizes of rooms vary, the smallest rooms at Dartmouth are generally the size of the biggest rooms at larger schools. People in the Choates and the River will have slightly smaller rooms than usual, but most other dorms have incredibly spacious rooms. East Wheelock, in particular, has gigantic rooms with terrific views. **Greek Houses also are an integral part in the housing situation,** and many Greek-associated people choose to reside in their respective houses."

The College Prowler Take On...
Campus Housing

Of Dartmouth's residential clusters, the Choates and the River are uniformly the regarded as the worst digs. However, the half of freshmen who are stuck there often say that the bonding experience of single-class housing makes up for the cramped quarters. River parties and the Choates' proximity to Frat Row aren't half bad either. East Wheelock has far and away the nicest dorms, although its students are known for their tee-totaling ways and 10 p.m. bedtimes. Freshman in mixed-class housing land frequently land spacious rooms in Wheeler-Richardson or New Hamp, and many get singles in Ripley-Woodward-Smith. Upper-class favorite Massachusetts Row cluster has the best location, while the recently renovated Gold Coast dorms are regarded as the nicest.

Dartmouth's community is made stronger by the fact that almost all Dartmouth students, even seniors, live on campus in dorms or Greek houses. And, with the spacious size of most dorms, it's easy to see why. Most residence halls are of equal quality, and none is more than a ten-minute walk from anywhere on campus. Students don't develop strong cluster allegiances, but placing freshman in the River and Choates may be a step toward a campus-wide residential college system. The competitiveness of sophomore room draw makes it hard to wind up near your friends and lands many students on the waitlist. However, while we can't guarantee you'll avoid that nightmare roommate, attending Dartmouth is good bet that you'll have a large enough room that you can keep your distance.

B+

The College Prowler™ Grade on
Campus Housing: B+

A high Campus Housing grade indicates that dorms are clean, well-maintained, and spacious. Other determining factors include variety of dorms, proximity to classes, and social atmosphere.

Off-Campus Housing

The Lowdown On...
Off-Campus Housing

Undergrads in Off-Campus Housing:

500-1000 (12-25%)

Average Rent for a 1BR:
$500-$700/month

Average Rent for a 2BR:
$600-$1000/month

Popular Areas:

Close to campus- School
Street and Lebanon Street.
Hot spots include:
8 School
7 West
30 Lebanon
the Red Barn
the Loveshack
the Moontowers

For Assistance Contact:
Dartmouth College Real Estate
Office

Web: http://www.dartmouthre.
com

Phone: (603) 646-2446

Best Time to Look for a Place:
As early as possible,
generally a year in advance.

Students Speak Out On...
Off-Campus Housing

"I know a bunch of people that've moved off campus. It seems pretty convenient, although I don't find it as practical as it would be at a big university. The dorms at Dartmouth are pretty good."

Q "Don't believe anyone who says there isn't a lot of it. **You can find housing in Hanover anywhere** as long as you're looking. I live off campus now for Sophomore Summer, and it's been fabulous."

Q "There really isn't much off campus housing, so **most people live in the dorms all four years at Dartmouth.** Some off-campus housing exists, of course, but nothing off campus is connected to the computer network, and that's a significant drawback."

Q **"It's sort of limited,** especially since the school is buying up a lot of off-campus apartments. I personally like the dorms, but I know a lot of people off campus who are happy with that."

Q **"It's great to live off campus** and feel more independent. You can cook your own meals, live with your closest friends, and get away from campus when things get stressful."

Q "Housing off-campus is usually pretty cool, but it goes quick, so **you need to plan in advance."**

Q "It is **very limited and relatively expensive.** Don't expect to have your own apartment."

Q "If you want to live off campus, it is a definite possibility after your freshman year, but **there's not a ton of housing in town** so you have to plan early. I actually have a house already for my junior year with nine other people. Usually off-campus housing is pretty nice—if you can get a place."

Q **"It's available to those who want it** for reasonable prices, but it's uncommon for people to want to leave campus. Frankly, there's not much reason to when the on-campus digs are so great."

Q "There isn't a lot of housing off campus because there isn't a lot off campus. (Hanover is pretty darn small.) **Cost will vary,** convenience will vary, and landlords are generally rotten but they vary, too.'"

Q **"Expensive,** though seldom more so than dorms."

The College Prowler Take On...
Off-Campus Housing

While many students live off campus for a term or two, especially during sophomore summer, there's no mass exodus from the dorms like at any many other schools. The choice between the apartments adjacent to campus and the bigger houses deep in Hanover comes down to whether or not students want to drive to school every day.

Off campus housing varies wildly in price and quality, as well as in distance from campus. The dorms are as nice as, or nicer than, most apartments and cost about the same on average. But because of changes in the College's blocking policy, however, it is difficult to live with a group of friends in the same dorm after freshman year. That is the main appeal of off campus houses - a chance to spend a lot of quality time with close friends in a secluded setting.

The College Prowler™ Grade on
Off-Campus
Housing: B

A high grade in Off-Campus Housing indicates that apartments are of high quality, close to campus, affordable, and easy to secure.

Diversity

The Lowdown On...
Diversity

American Indian:
3.0%

**Asian or Pacific
Islander:**
11.7%

African American:
6.2%

Hispanic:
6.5%

White:
59.6%

International:
4.8%

Unknown:
8.1%

Out of State:
97%

Political Activity

While the conservative *Dartmouth Review* is an established institution and the relatively new *Dartmouth Free Press* has added a liberal perspective to the campus debate, most students are apathetic. However, since New Hampshire is the first primary state, all Dartmouth students are guaranteed to get an up close view of at least one Presidential election and a slew of visits from chief executive hopefuls, generating a political buzz once every four years.

Gay Tolerance

Out students fare quite well, while those still in the closet often have a tougher time. Gays are becoming more prominent on campus, and acceptance is generally growing.

Most Popular Religions

Catholics, Muslims, Jews, and Protestants of several denominations have a presense on campus, while the non-denominational Tucker Foundation ensures that all faiths are respected and acknowledged. Only a small minority of Dartmouth students practice their religions fervently.

Economic Status

That half aren't on any financial aid speaks to the general wealth of Dartmouth students. But despite the Ivy League prestige, there is little old money at Dartmouth- few affluent students flaunt their wealth or act in an elitist manner. There are many middle class students partially working their way through college, although there are few working class students.

Minority Clubs

AfriCaSO, Dartmouth Asian Organization, Dartmouth Chinese Culture Society, Hokupa'a, International Students Association, Japan Society, Korean American Students Association, La Alianza Latina, Movimiento Estudiantil Chicano/a de Aztlan), MOSAIC, Native Americans at Dartmouth, Shamis, Vietnamese Student Association

Students Speak Out On...
Diversity

"Well, campus is very white. There are minorities of all kinds: gay, black, Indian, Native American, Hispanic, Jewish, etc. Dartmouth is actually the most diverse school I've ever been to, but I think that after 200-plus years of being a predominantly white, heterosexual male environment, the college still has some work to do on improving life for minorities. They need to create an environment in which everyone around you is unique in their personality, yet similar as far as intellectual values."

"People complain a lot about Dartmouth not being diverse. In some ways, this complaint is completely justified. In others ways, I think people are missing what is around them. **I have friends of all different races, ethnicities, and backgrounds,** and diversity at Dartmouth has been essential to my positive experience here."

"This is a tough question to answer, because, even though the College is numerically very diverse, I think the administration has gone about it in exactly the wrong way. The notion communicated from above is that I should make up for centuries of white male privilege by feeling guilty and being sensitive. While changing with the times certainly in order, **I think the College is really losing its identity** in a sea of politically-correct mumbo jumbo."

Q "**Dartmouth is approaching a 40%/60% minority/ non-minority ratio** and has improved in the area of diversity by leaps and bounds. Despite a small natural minority recruiting pool (New Hampshire is one of the whitest states in the nation), Dartmouth has succeeded in bringing people of different races, ethnicities, religions, and perspectives together for an explosion of discourse. While racial self-segregation is a minor problem at the College, students consciously identify artificial barriers to relationships (like race) and act to overcome them."

Q "While very few people are 100% free of preconceived notions at Dartmouth (just as in most other areas of the world), **Dartmouth students take advantage of their diversity** in exploring new intellectual and personal areas together."

Q "**Some people say that Dartmouth is 'too white,'** but it's more diverse than my high school was. It's all relative."

Q "**As far as being gay at Dartmouth, I find the school to be unacceptable.** I could talk about this for a while, but just know that, as a minority, I don't feel like Dartmouth is doing as much as they can for me. With the 2 billion dollar endowment that the school has, you'd think they could do more."

Q "**We're not a particularly diverse campus.** We have quite a few international students, but I don't find the place to be very diverse."

Q "Diversity is a problem that the college is addressing now. Personally **I think the campus is diverse—some think otherwise,** but I have friends from all races and a whole bunch of foreign countries."

Q "It's not as diverse as most of the other Ivy League schools, so **it could be better.**"

Q "I guess we've got plenty of it, and the administration is very committed to it, for better or worse. Don't let its 'conservative' reputation fool you; **Dartmouth is a very liberal place.** Achieving their idealized notion of diversity ranks high among the administration's priorities."

Q "It's not super diverse, or at least people complain sometimes that it isn't. **There are quite a few foreign students,** though."

Q **"The campus is very diverse.** The class of 2006 has a very high percentage of people of color and in general, you'll find a lot of different ethnic backgrounds, economic backgrounds, and diverse ideas on campus."

Q "On an individual level, **students mix very well** and have friends of all races. However, I there is a decent amount of group racial tension."

Q **"You're bound to meet many different types of people,** whether you classify them by categories of diversity or not. Students complain that it can be cliquish, though I didn't have that experience."

Q "Total conjecture on my part, but I think Dartmouth's failure to attract the super-brilliant kids that go to Yale and Harvard prevent the school from being as socio-economically and ideologically diverse as it could be. That being said, **everybody's friendly and welcoming,** even if many are rich and from New York."

The College Prowler Take On...
Diversity

As an Ivy League institution, Dartmouth has a centuries-old tradition of being straight, white, and male. Despite fervent administration efforts to promote diversity, the "average" Dartmouth students are still crusty New England types sporting Northface. Special programs abound for traditionally underrepresented groups. Efforts to recruit American Indians, whom Dartmouth was originally founded to educate, have been particularly vigorous. Students also report a sizable international population on campus.

While women and minorities are now proportionally represented on campus, many still feel like outsiders in the rugged New Hampshire woods. Meanwhile, other students feel racial minorities frequently self-segregate into "affinity housing" and homogenous Greek houses. Race notwithstanding, Dartmouth is still dominated by upper-middle-class students from the East Coast, although most students mix easily with friends from all regions and socioeconomic statuses. Despite occasional tension, a strong sense of school spirit often prevails over individual differences.

The College Prowler™ Grade on
Diversity: C+

A high grade in Diversity indicates that ethnic minorities and international students have a notable presence on campus and that students of different economic backgrounds, religious beliefs, and sexual preferences are well-represented.

Guys & Girls

The Lowdown On...
Guys & Girls

Men Undergrads:
51.1%

Women Undergrads:
48.9%

Birth Control Available?
Yes

Most Prevalent STDs on Campus:
Gonorrhea, Chlamydia

Percentage of Students with an STD:
Allegedly 40%, including latent cases, but this number is controversial.

Social Scene:

With no notable divisions among its student body, Dartmouth has a vibrant social scene. While some students initiate love affairs with their laptops and others go out every night of the week, most know when to hit the books and when to let loose—usually two or three nights each seven days. Students are usually very friendly in classes and extracurricular activities. As opportunities to meet others abound in daily interactions and most students are linked by about two degrees of separation, building an ample social network is often as easy as lingering in the dining halls. While people usually associate by degrees of coolness, and the strength of athletes' bonds tends to make them exclusive groups, most students do have a wide cross-section of casual friends.

Hookups or Relationships?

Commitment-free hookups are extremely prevalent, to the frustration of many guys and girls. Those who enter relationships often do so seriously, to the point that casual dinner-and-movie relations are about as common as pterodactyls around campus. Many students enter Dartmouth with hometown significant others, but most of these relationships quickly fade away.

Best Place to Meet Guys/Girls:

Most hookups are initiated at weekend parties. Many students are acquainted with their "random" partner from an activity or through a mutual friend and use alcohol to bypass that extensive, unnecessary "getting-to-know" stage. The campus is small enough that you can see your crush almost every day with minimal effort. Extracurricular activities are a great way to expand your pool of friends, which becomes a pool of potential hookup partners come Friday night. Beer pong (played with paddles, unlike Beirut), is used universally as a poor man's date.

As with birds, grass, and everything else, relationships tend to blossom anew come spring. Everybody becomes infinitely hotter when all that winter clothing is shed. Studly men and buxom ladies summarily trot out to the Green to study, toss a Frisbee, and flash their hot bods.

Top Places to Hookup:

There are seven places that you have to hit before graduation.

1. BEMA (Big Empty Meeting Area)
2. Baker Stacks
3. Football Field- 50 Yard Line.
4. The Green
5. Top of the Hop
6. President Wright's Lawn
7. The Graveyard

Dress Code

The protocol definitely calls for preppy, although with a North Woods twist. One glance at the Hinman Box mailroom indicates that J. Crew is the manufacturer of choice, but be sure to bring along that North Face or Columbia for when the weather turns cold. While students may throw on jeans and a decent sweater for class, they don't overdo it. That goes for parties as well, over which guys and girls rarely fuss – and who could blame them, with a night of mucky basements and a disinclination to remember ahead. Moreover, when it's time for one of many theme parties, dress codes go out the window. Color Dartmouth students "refined outdoorsy."

Did You Know?
Top Places to Find Hotties:
1. The Green in Spring
2. Webster Ave. on Wed., Fri., or Sat.
3. Kresge Fitness Center Weekday Afternoons

Students Speak Out On...
Guys & Girls

"It's hard to generalize when it comes to looks. I think that the 'stereotypical' Dartmouth male would be a beer-guzzling football-playing frat boy, but you will find that the guys are all very different. I consider myself to be as far from the 'typical' Dartmouth male as possible. The girls are the same way—the stereotypical girl would be a ditzy blonde sorority girl, but obviously they're not all that way. Both the guys and the girls are pretty attractive, I'd say. All in all, we have a good looking campus."

Q "Everyone says the girls aren't that hot, but **I think they're the same as at other colleges.** They just wear more clothing because it is cold in Hanover a lot of the time."

Q "**The guys here are not too bad.** There are plenty of attractive, driven men for any girl to be pleased. Whether or not you'll actually form a meaningful relationship is a completely different question."

Q "Supposedly the guys are 'above average' (I have had girls tell me this), and the girls are 'below average' (all the guys I know agree). **The girls are not so hot,** but then again, Dartmouth isn't a state school, so this is to be expected."

Q "Overall, I would say **it's a pretty decent looking student body.**"

Q "**Nice, cute, fun guys are everywhere,** but the campus seems to fall into two categories when it comes to dating: random hook-ups that leave people confused, hurt, and make for awkward situations, but can be a lot of fun; and the married-since-they-met crowd, which couples up and tends to live together. There doesn't seem to be a middle ground of adult dating. Meeting a guy through friend or in class, an activity, etc., seems to lead to more successful relationships than drunken hook-ups with near-strangers."

Q "Well, it's a mixed bag. **We tend to attract a ton of athletic girls,** so we get a mix of hyper-attractive athletes and relatively unattractive 'butch women.' The good thing is that they're generally all confident, smart, witty, and classy. Although dating can be difficult in the party-oriented atmosphere, it is comforting to know that it's easy to make friends with girls no matter what they look like."

Q "The **guys are pretty cool and laid back and love to party.** The girls are pretty cool, but usually way below par in looks, which really sucks."

Q "Dartmouth **girls are generally regarded as some of the ugliest in the Ivy League.** Lookers are few and tend to be snapped up by jocks and frat boys. The almost exactly equal gender ratio destroys any advantage guys would normally have in dating, and the result is almost cutthroat competition. Still, there are diamonds to be found in the rough."

Q "**Everybody is really nice and smart.** I happen to think the guys are very good-looking."

Q "Guys are much more attractive than average, and **girls have really been on the rise** since the inception of the Dartmouth Beautification Project, a little-known program that means to increase student happiness by only admitting the most attractive of qualified applicants."

The College Prowler Take On...
Guys & Girls

Don't drop that high school sweetheart just yet, but Dartmouth students seem to think they look all right. The disparity between guys and girls is very real, although recent female classes are quickly closing the gap, regardless of whether or not the Dartmouth Beautification Project actually exists. Hookups—drunken or otherwise—dominate a virtually nonexistent dating scene. Most students are able to locate a hottie or two, though sometimes a pair of beer goggles is required.

While Ivy Leaguers are known more for brain than brawn, Dartmouth students defy the stereotype. Students in general and freshman guys in particular sometimes complain about the slim pickings, but most everyone is relatively normal looking, not to mention in fantastic shape. However, if Hanover winters weren't depressing enough, just imagine trying to determine who's hot under all that clothing.

The College Prowler™ Grade on
Guys: A-

A high grade for Guys indicates that the male population on campus is attractive, smart, friendly, and engaging, and that the school has a decent ratio of guys to girls.

The College Prowler™ Grade on
Girls: B-

A high grade for Girls not only implies that the women on campus are attractive, smart, friendly, and engaging, but also that there is a fair ratio of girls to guys.

Athletics

The Lowdown On...
Athletics

Athletic Division:
NCCA Division I
(I-AA for Men's Football)

Conference:
Eastern College Athletic
Conference

Men's Varsity Sports:
Baseball
Basketball
Crew, Lightweight
Crew, Heavyweight
Cross Country (plus JV team)
Football (plus JV team)
Golf
Ice Hockey
Lacrosse
Skiing, Alpine and Cross
Country
Soccer (plus JV team)
Squash
Swimming and Diving
Tennis
Track and Field

Women's Varsity Sports:
Basketball
Crew (plus Novice team)
Cross Country (plus JV team)
Field Hockey
Golf
Ice Hockey
Lacrosse
Skiing, Alpine & Cross Country
Soccer (plus JV team)
Softball
Squash
Swimming and Diving
Tennis
Track and Field
Volleyball

Club Sports:
Badminton
Biathlon
Boxing
Cheerleading, Football
Cricket, Men's
Cycling
Dressage
EMS
Fencing
Figure Skating
Ice Hockey
Pom
Rugby
Snowboarding
Table Tennis
Tae Kwan Do
Tang Soo Doo
Tennis, Women's
Triathlon
Ultimate Frisbee,Volleyball, Men's
Water Polo
Wresting

Intramurals:
Basketball
Eight Ball
Free Throw Shooting
Flag Football
Golf Handball
Ice Hockey
Lacrosse
Racquetball
Ski Races
Soccer
Softball
Squash
Table Tennis
Tennis/Team Tennis
Turkey Trot Fun Run
Volleyball
Wallyball
Water Polo
Whiffle Ball

Coed Teams:
Equestrian
Sailing

Physical Education:

Ballroom Dance
Basketball
Fencing
First Aid/CPR
Fitness (FLIP)
Fly Fishing
Goju-Ryu Karate
Golf
Horseback Riding Ice Skating
Ice Hockey
JuJitsu & Aikido
Mountain Biking
Kayaking
Learning at Dartmouth
Peer Health Education
Polocrosse
Racquetball Rape Awareness/
Defense
Red Cross Lifeguard
Rock Climbing
Sailing
Scuba Diving
Skiing: Alpine
Skiing: Nordic
Snowboarding
Snowshoe Hiking Squash
Swimming
Tae Kwon Do
Tai Chi
Tennis
Tumbling
Volleyball
Wellness Works

Number of Males Playing Varsity Sports:

441

Percent of Males Playing Varsity Sports:

15%

Number of Females Playing Varsity Sports:

442

Percent of Females Playing Varsity Sports:

17%

Athletic Fields

Memorial Field
Sachem Field
Scully-Fahey Field

School Mascot
None

School Nickname:
Big Green

Getting Tickets
All students receive free entry to all sporting events simply by flashing their IDs. Additional planning is unnecessary.

Most Popular Sports
Men's rugby, football, and both ice hockey teams have the largest following. Rugby, crew, and ultimate frisbee all have large squads.

Overlooked Teams:
Women's basketball had a solid yet overlooked season, while, at the club level, the cycling team is fantastic.

Best Place to Take a Walk
Occom Pond, Golf Course

Gyms/Facilities

Alumni Gym
The primary exercise facility for non-athletes (NCAA competitors frequent Davis Varsity House), Alumni Gyms and the adjoining Berry Sports Center contain squash and basketball courts, a pool, and a weightlifting facility (Kresge Fitness Center). Additionally, the gym complex houses Leede Arena, home court of the Big Green basketball squads.

Leverone Field House
The chief indoor facility on campus includes a track and batting cages.

Thompson Arena

This 3,500-seat hockey arena is occasionally open for free skating.

Dartmouth Skiway

Just a short drive from campus, the Skiway boasts a three lifts, sixteen trains, and a lodge.

Hanover Country Club

Scenic golf course adjacent to campus.

Tennis Courts

Six indoor courts compose the Boss Center, while an additional seventeen courts, four or them clay, are part of Dartmouth's athletic facilities.

Boathouses

Allen Boathouse, home of the sailing team, adjoins Lake Mascoma, while the Friends of Dartmouth Rowing Boathouse is on the Connecticut River.

Students Speak Out On...
Athletics

{ **"Varsity sports are huge at Dartmouth; tons of people are involved in sports some way."**

 "The varsity sports are not so big. If you're looking for a school where athletics are an integral part of campus life, then Dartmouth isn't going to be your first choice. IM sports exist, but they aren't huge."

"The main draws are football and hockey, although we have great success in several other areas, including nationally-ranked lacrosse and crew teams. **Our football team draws huge crowds,** especially for the Homecoming and Harvard games. While our teams, as of late, have not been terribly successful, a good time is had by all. With hockey, on the other hand, Dartmouth has seen a great deal of success."

"Our women's team has been ranked in the top 10 nationally for several years and makes regular appearances in the last stages of the NCAA tournament. **Club and intramural sports are enormously popular,** with nearly all students participating in some type of athletics."

"Athletes are a dominant force on campus. The resulting furor when the administration tried to cut the swim team far exceeded the mumbles of discontent over the closing of satellite libraries. While hockey comes close, there is no dominant sport on campus...but people here are always exercising. Sometimes I wonder if the admissions office specifically rejects obese people."

Q "Some sports are big—soccer comes to mind. We suck at football right now so that's not huge. **Hockey is all right.** I guess it really depends if you're a diehard fan. We lose a lot, so it's hard to keep interest high. Skiing is also big, obviously."

Q "A lot of student are athletes, and those who aren't are very supportive. **We have much to offer in this area,** so be prepared to take advantage."

Q "**IM sports are very fun** if they can rally enough members and support. Frats and sororities often participate in those."

Q "**Girls sports seem to be doing better** at the intercollegiate level as of late."

Q "Some sports are better then other, but no matter how badly the football team does (and it is usually bloody awful), **there's always a big audience at games.** IM sports are popular; most organizations have their own teams—College Bowl's basketball team or the 'Godsquad' in softball, a combination of Aquinas House (Catholic organization) and Hillel."

Q "**Take advantage of the PE classes** to learn skills you probably won't acquire later in life."

Q "I think having an intangible mascot like 'Big Green' helps keep people from getting really excited about sports. **There's talk of getting a new nickname,** but we'll see if that ever happens."

Q "My Dartmouth interviewer told me that he knew only a few people who weren't involved in sports in some way. I've certainly found that to be, **even if we don't have many teams** that the whole school rallies behind."

The College Prowler Take On...
Athletics

Very few students watch Dartmouth sporting events religiously, but don't let that fool into thinking they can't distinguish between football and futbol. This small school supports an amazing number of NCAA teams, meaning that a full half of Dartmouth students are varsity athletes. While basketball and football haven't fielded dominant teams for years, but winter hockey games at Leverone Field House are a favorite.

There is sometimes a divide between athletes and their egghead peers, but all the sweating that goes on at Dartmouth generally promotes a friendly atmosphere friendly for the student-athlete. Even students not on a varsity squad are usually very active. Some play intramurals, while others join popular club teams like rugby, crew, and ultimate Frisbee. Additionally, most hike, ski, or otherwise enjoy the great outdoors.

The College Prowler™ Grade on

Athletics: B+

A high grade in Athletics indicates that students have school spirit, that sports programs are respected, that games are well-attended, and that intramurals are a prominent part of student life.

Nightlife

The Lowdown On...
Nightlife

Club and Bar Prowler:
Popular Nightlife Spots!

Club Crawler:
None

Bar Prowler:
5 Olde Nugget Alley
5 Olde Nugget Alley, Hanover

(603) 643-5081

Other Places to Check Out:
Murphy's
Molly's
Seven Barrel
(see Off Campus Dining)

What to Do if You're Not 21:
Catch a movie or hit the frats

Favorite Drinking Games:

Beer Pong- This game differs from Beer Pong at most schools, as it is played with paddles. The object is to arc the ball into your opponents cups. It also involves considerably more drinking than Beruit, which involves throwing.

Dice- (also known as 7-11-Doubles)

Organization Parties:

While most College-sanctioned parties are thoroughly lame (especially if at FUEL), cultural events in Collis Commonground or elsewhere can be a decent night-starter.

Frats:

See the Greek Section!

Students Speak Out On...
Nightlife

> **"There aren't many bars or clubs. Murphy's is a good bar at night."**

Q "I think **there's one club in the area,** but it's probably a joke. New Hampshire isn't really the 'hippest' place on earth. Same goes for bars. The restaurants in Hanover have bars, but that's about it."

Q **"A few places around town turn into bars around 10 p.m.** If you're 21+, they're a lot of fun. If not, the only real option is Greek houses and private parties. Generally, private parties are more fun, but some whole houses have that feeling."

Q "Unfortunately, Hanover is small, and **there are no clubs in the area.** The bars are anal about underage drinking, so not many people hang out there, however, the fraternities make up for the lack of town nightlife."

Q "It's Hanover. There are no bars or clubs anywhere nearby. Instead there are frats. **We do, however, have Lone Pine Tavern in Collis,** which serves alcohol to people of age and has pretty good food."

Q "As for bars and clubs, there really aren't any. **It's really rural.**"

Q "No clubs. **There are a couple bars** but mostly the Greek system (frats and sororities) is the source of nightlife. There are sponsored concerts there and parties every weekend sponsored by the frats and sororities themselves, and they take the place of clubs. However, the Greek system is under attack right now, things may change."

Q "There are none in Hanover. **That's what frat row is for."**

Q "For those that don't like the party scene, **there are always cool events to go to.** Dartmouth attracts a lot of interesting speakers. I've seen Ehud Barak, Bishop Desmond Tutu, Alison Brown, Charles Ogletree, etc. Oh, and tomorrow some NASA astronauts are coming to speak about their past mission repairing the Hubble space telescope. There are music groups, plays, comedians, and other things to hear all the time... Two weeks ago I got to see Itzhak Perlman for only five bucks! :) A capella is also very popular on campus."

Q **"The nightlife is mainly focused on the fraternity scene,** although the campus provides strong supplements and alternatives. Options include free or extremely inexpensive movies, free food options, discussion groups, speakers, pool and billiards, and more."

Q "On campus entertainment, varies from decent to awful. **This year, I caught a couple of offbeat movies** like Dogtown and Z-Boys and a documentary about Jerry Seinfeld, which were pretty cool. For those of age, Lone Pine is a decent place to grab a drink if you're of age, but Fuel Nightclub is beyond lame, as are most College-sponsored parties."

Q **"Every person who has come to visit me has had a blast at night.** There is a lot to do (considering our location), and people seldom complain about options. It's more common to hear people whine about having too much work to go out."

The College Prowler Take On...
Nightlife

Bars are extremely rare, save for 5 Olde and restaurants. You'll also have to hold that groove thang, as clubs are non-existent off the golf course. Most weekends will feature a house party or two, although they are often hit or miss and require a long walk down Lebanon Street. Unless you count a NASA lecture as a party, must school-sponsored events don't pass muster, although a capella shows do attract sizable crowds. It is worth noting that Dartmouth is one of the few colleges in the country where fake IDs are entirely unnecessary. Anyone who wants beer can get it at fraternities, where there is no carding- and it's easy to find an upper classmen to go on a liquor run to West Lebanon.

As with Hanover in general, no nightlife exists apart from Dartmouth, parties or otherwise. While it's sometimes fun just to chill in the dorms with your friends, be prepared to swill beer in frat basements if you venture out for entertainment.

D

The College Prowler™ Grade on
Nightlife: D

A high grade in Nightlife indicates that there are many bars and clubs in the area that are easily accessible and affordable. Other determining factors include the number of options for the under-21 crowd and the prevalence of house parties.

Greek Life

The Lowdown On...
Greek Life

Number of Fraternities:
17

Number of Sororities:
10

Number of Coed Houses:
3

Number of Undergraduate Societies:
2

Percent of Undergrad Men in Fraternities:
28% of men, 37% of eligible men (non-freshmen)

Percent of Undergrad Women in Sororities:
22% of women, 30% of eligible women (non-freshmen)

➜

Fraternities on Campus:

Psi Upsilon (national)

Kappa Kappa Kappa (local)

Alpha Delta (local)

Zeta Psi (national; permanently derecognized by College)

Theta Delta Chi (national)

Phi Delta Alpha (local)

Chi Heorot (local)

Bones Gate (local)

Sigma Nu (national)

Sigma Alpha Epsilon (national)

Chi Gamma Epsilon (local)

Gamma Delta Chi (local)

Sigma Phi Epsilon (national)

Alpha Chi Alpha (local; non-residential)

Alpha Phi Alpha (national; non-residential)

Kappa Alpha Psi (national; non-residential)

Lambda Upsilon Lambda (national; non-residential)

Sororities on Campus:

Sigma Delta (local)

Kappa Kappa Gamma (national)

Epsilon Kappa Theta (local)

Alpha Kappa Alpha (national; non-residential)

Delta Sigma Theta (national; non-residential)

Delta Delta Delta (national)

Kappa Delta Epsilon (local)

Alpha Xi Delta (national)

Sigma Lambda Upsilon (national; non-residential)

Alpha Pi Omega (national; non-residential)

Coed Houses:

Phi Tau (local)

Alpha Theta (local)

The Tabard (local)

Undergraduate Societies:

Panarchy

Amarna

Other Greek Organizations:

Greek Leaders Council, Interfraternity Council, Panhellenic Council, Pan-Hellenic Council, Coed Council

Did You Know?

• **Animal House writer** Chris Miller based the famous Delta chapter after Dartmouth's own Alpha Delta.

Students Speak Out On...
Greek Life

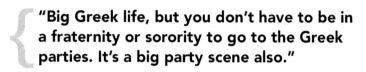

"Big Greek life, but you don't have to be in a fraternity or sorority to go to the Greek parties. It's a big party scene also."

"Most houses can be stereotyped, but there are many exceptions to each rule. Greeks provide most of the social space and programming on campus outside of college-sponsored events (which tend to be lackluster). Come with an open mind—I never planned to be Greek and I ended up running a fraternity!"

"Greek Life = Party Life. The Greek like is pretty big on campus, although I'm not affiliated. I don't really think there's a lot of pressure one way or the other, it all depends on what you like. The administration is trying to do away with the fraternity/sorority system now, but that won't come about anytime soon."

"Frats are the dominant social scene on campus. Despite the presence of sororities and co-ed organizations, **when people go out on the weekends, they go to frats.** You can find somewhere to party at any time on any night of the week. I nearly didn't come to Dartmouth because of the strength of the Greek system, but now I'm glad I did. While I came on to campus as a freshman vowing to never join a frat, I found out that their reputations are generally ill-deserved."

"While the parties are fun, the camaraderie and closeness that develops between members is incredible and well worth the disgust from looking at the floors of the basements. **The Greek system is one of the last remnants of Old Dartmouth,** the way that college life was supposed to be."

Q "As for social life, what you do in Hanover on a Friday night revolves around your friends. **Generally my freshman year had a lot of drinking and stuff.** The frats play good music; no matter what kind of music you like, you can find it somewhere. They're sleazy, but I don't mind them that much."

Q "Not as bad as some would initially think. **Houses are vastly different from one another** and change every year. Sorority rush is awful, but it's worth the outcome of fifty to eighty potential new friends and a place that you're always welcome."

Q **"Greek life doesn't dominate campus life** as much as people think. If you want nothing to do with the frats, you can lead an equally exciting life without becoming involved."

Q **"It can be overwhelming** and all-encompassing at times, but it's a great social option if you choose to join a house or attend events. There is a sense that everyone and anyone on campus is welcome, so openness is a positive feature.'"

Q "I'll admit that **the Greek system is a huge part of Dartmouth,** but it doesn't dominate the social scene. Parties are either in dorms, the frats, or in off-campus apartments. Personally, I plan to rush a fraternity this term."

Q **"Greek life on campus is very influential,** and many men and women decide to become affiliated with a Greek organization. Alcohol often plays a role in Greek life and activities. However, to say that this is a defining characteristic of Greeks is untrue. Greek houses frequently sponsor community service opportunities, concerts, speakers, and other community-oriented events. Greek life at Dartmouth also serves to foster community by increasing the support network available to students."

Q "There are parties every weekend on frat row. It's a pretty substantial part of Dartmouth's social life, but **I personally don't partake very often.** Only on big party weekends. My friends and I manage to find other things to do with our time."

Q "The Greek system is huge at Dartmouth. Like half of eligible students are in Greek houses, and that surely does dominate the social scene. If you're not into that, there's other stuff to do. So instead of going out to bars and stuff, we hang out at fraternities and sororities. **The drinks are always free,** and you can find a dance party almost every weekend. The majority of students are out partying on the weekends."

Q "There are a few bars, but since I am not 21 and don't have a fake ID, I mostly go to frats or parties at off-campus houses. The frat parties are pretty fun. **The basements are usually nasty** but with lots of free beer, and upstairs there are usually dance parties and other fun stuff. I'd say the Greek scene dominates the drinking scene, but there are certainly people who go to frats and don't drink, and there is always other stuff to do if you are not into the frat scene."

Q "The Greek system dominates; a large percentage of the student body is a member of a frat or sorority. The campus is completely rural, so without any clubs people go to frat parties. Wednesday, Friday, and Saturday are the biggest nights. They're fun but completely informal. **Usually, it's dancing and DJ upstairs, beer pong downstairs.**"

Q "There are **always parties going on every weekend** as well as Wednesday nights. That doesn't necessarily mean drinking, but it does for a large number of students. Some students go just for the music or dancing. 80s at Sigma Nu and Disco Inferno at The Tabard are favorites each term."

The College Prowler Take On...
Greek Life

As far as parties go, it's all Greek to me. While half of eligible students—those in their sophomore fall or later—pledge a fraternity or sorority, you don't have to be Greek to partake. Almost all frat parties are open to all students, and cheap beer—Keystone—flows freely to all. Liquor is less common, although invite–only "'tails" events are popular. Beer pong is the official Dartmouth sport, but most weekend nights feature at least once dance party. Students may drink like fish, but even those on the wagon frequent frats to socialize with their friends. And even for abstaining students, the parties on big weekends are truly a sight to behold.

While the days of Animal House can be relived only on celluloid, Greek houses dominate the social scene. The frats remain an entrenched part of Dartmouth culture, despite administration efforts to diminish their influence though an ineffectual Student Life Initiative. While a few students don't care for the frats and some upperclassmen grow weary of the monotonous scene, the Greek system is a binding tie for most. Three nights a week, most of action can still be found on good ole' Webster Ave.

The College Prowler™ Grade on
Greek Life: A

A high grade in Greek Life indicates that sororities and fraternities are not only present, but also active on campus. Other determining factors include the variety of houses available and the respect the Greek community receives from the rest of the campus.

Drug Scene

The Lowdown On...
Drug Scene

Most Prevalent Drugs on Campus:
Marijuana
Ecstasy
Cocaine

Liquor-Related Arrests:
Campus Safety and Security reported 247 cases of alcohol related arrests last year.

Drug-Related Arrests:
Not listed

Drug Counseling Programs
Counseling and Human Development

Phone: (603) 650-1442

Services: Assessment
Individual Counseling
Group Counseling

Students Speak Out On...
Drug Scene

"Not much of one that I know of. If you want drugs, you can certainly get them, but it's not a huge deal at Dartmouth, and I think most students like it that way."

Q "I know that there's pot, and **every once in a while there's ecstasy.** I don't know much about the drug scene, though, I only dabble here and there."

Q **"If you aren't into drugs, you won't know they're there**. If you want drugs, you'll always be able to find them."

Q "They're basically nonexistent. **There's a little weed here and there** and a few other drugs, but you have to actively look for drugs other than pot to find them. I partied frequently last year and only saw alcohol, weed, and one piece of mushrooms. Nothing more."

Q **"Drugs aren't that big on campus,** maybe weed and ecstasy, if you look around a bit, but you have to look really hard to find anything harder. Also, some fraternities have reputations for different things."

Q **"The two biggest drugs are pot and ecstasy.** Quite a few people smoke up, but it's not a big deal. Personally, I don't smoke, and I have never been pressured into smoking at Dartmouth."

Q "Lots of pot, other substances can be found if you're good at networking. **Relatively low-key."**

Q "Drugs exist, but **they aren't a big issue** on campus."

Q **"I don't do them, but others do.** That's about all I know."

Q "I don't think there are a lot of drugs at Dartmouth. **There's much more alcohol** than drugs."

Q **"The drug scene is pretty low key;** but it does exist. Most people stick to alcohol, although I've seen tons of pot, and ecstasy is starting to become popular."

Q "Drugs are surprisingly present, despite the remoteness of Hanover. **Hard drugs are available,** though you won't witness much unless you specifically seek them, so it's easy to avoid. Most people aren't into it."

Q **"I don't do drugs,** so I wouldn't know—drinking seems to be the bigger activity at Dartmouth."

Q "It's there but doesn't influence the campus very much. Not many people use drugs, **it's mostly just drinkers. BIG drinkers**."

Q "One of my roommates was a dealer, so **I saw a bunch of weed,** but not much else."

The College Prowler Take On...
Drug Scene

While the average student may run across quite a bit of pot, Dartmouth's drug scene has a very low profile. While ecstasy or the occasional mushrooms might show up at parties, students generally pass on everything but the grass.

People in the know claim that the hard drugs are out there, and certain fraternities at Dartmouth have a reputation as substance abuse hot spots. While it may not satisfy the authorities or your parents, the most students are not bothered by the softer drugs they encounter.

B

The College Prowler™ Grade on
Drug Scene: B

A high grade in the Drug Scene indicates that drugs are not a noticeable part of campus life; drug use is not visible, and no pressure to use them seems to exist.

Campus Strictness

The Lowdown On...
Campus Strictness

What Are You Most Likely to Get Caught Doing on Campus?

- Public intoxication
- Drinking underage
- Having an unregistered keg
- Creating a fire hazard (read: leaving anything) in the hallway
- Keeping books from the reserve desk for too long
- Engaging in a vicious "blitz" war
- Streaking across the Green
- Speaking your politically incorrect mind

Students Speak Out On...
Campus Strictness

"They're not very strict. If you get really sick from drinking and have to go to the medical center, you won't get in trouble. I don't think they bust down on drugs very much because it would make Dartmouth look bad and heaven forbid that happen. I've never had a problem with either. If need be, though, Safety and Security will call in the Hanover Police."

Q "If you don't act very drunk or stoned, **there's generally not a problem.** Don't let them see you drink or do drugs, don't get caught with paraphernalia, and you should be fine."

Q "Lots of people get picked up by Safety and Security when they're drunk, but it's not a big deal, really. **Just make sure you don't get caught twice,** and your parents will never know."

Q "**Police try to be strict,** but drinking is a huge phenomenon at Dartmouth and it's impossible to curb it."

Q "Safety and Security officers are pretty cool with things. If you keep it inside, **they usually leave you alone,** but if you're stupid enough to stumble around campus, they'll nail you."

Q "Punishment for drinking can be severe depending on what campus police officer you get in trouble with. **You aren't thrown in jail for underage drinking,** everyone knows what goes on in frats, and campus police just need to make sure no one is seriously in danger, or else they get in trouble."

Q "If you're caught for underage drinking you must speak to the class Dean, and possibly they talk to your parents, you get a fine, I don't know. I was never caught. Hanover police are different story: **they suck.** They are less frequent than the ubiquitous Dartmouth campus police, luckily."

Q "While frats aren't supposed to serve minors, **the wristband system they use is a joke.** When Safety and Security walks into a party, people just calmly put down their drinks until they leave. However, while rules aren't so strict for individuals, frats have to jump through a ridiculous number of administrative hurdles to throw a party and often get in trouble for minor violations."

Q "If you're in bad shape, friends can 'Good Samaritan' you. Safety and Security will take you to Dick's House without getting you in trouble. While you only used to be allowed one time, **rules have recently been changed**."

Q "For the most part, there's not much strictness on campus. **Students generally do what they please** (within the bounds of the law) and have a great time doing it. Safety and Security usually stays out of students' business, except for when they're intervening for somebody's safety. While S&S has a bad rep in some quarters of campus, most people believe that S&S maintains a very low level of campus strictness while ensuring campus-wide safety."

Q "**The thought police are out in full force.** Dartmouth has a 'Principle of Community,' which a small minority, backed by the administration, use to keep people in line. Campus publications supposedly can no longer be delivered door-to-door starting this fall, and adjudication hearings for violations can be arbitrary and lopsided."

Q "**Getting worse.** I miss the keg jump."

Q "**The administration is very lax generally**—no attempts to enforce morals or anything like that—but comes down hard on the Greeks when they screw up. What can get you in trouble for is speaking your mind, assuming you are of the wrong (read: conservative) opinion."

Q "**This campus is not strict.** Not at all."

Q "**I got fined for everything** last year. Leaving shoes outside my door, unspecified hall damage, turning in my practice room key too late. It got to be rather ridiculous."

Q "The campus tries to be strict, but **you can get away with anything.**"

The College Prowler Take On...
Campus Strictness

Opinions are clearly mixed, but students most frequently encounter campus authorities while inebriated. While visibly soused students are frequently detained, Safety and Security usually won't bug those who act sober. While they conduct walkthroughs at parties, S&S looks the other way at mass underage drinking, so long as containers are kept inside. Detox trips to "Dick's House" involve a fine and a chat with a dean, but, unless hitchhiking from the Grafton County Jail is your idea of Sunday morning fun, stay away from the Hanover Police. Older students report that increasing administration exercise of in loco parentis is just plain loco and depriving Dartmouth of valuable traditions. Gone is the rope swing, as well as Psi Upsilon fraternity's keg jump.

While the administration rarely sweats the small stuff, fines for everything from parking violations to leaving shoes in the hall are annoying. The powers that be have also attempted to debilitate the Greek system through increasing strictness, banning kegs and placing all but a handful on probation for minor violations. More troublingly, politically correct buzzwords often dominate the exercise of free speech. Despite the unending list of rules, regulations, and violations, though, a remotely savvy student can get away with most forms of illegal activity. The bulk of the college's disciplinary weight falls on organizations (usually Greek) as opposed to individuals.

B

The College Prowler™ Grade on
Campus Strictness: B

A high Campus Strictness grade implies an overall lenient atmosphere; police and RAs are fairly tolerant, and the administration's rules are flexible.

Parking

The Lowdown On...
Parking

Approximate Parking Permit Cost

Student Parking Lot? A-Lot

Freshman Allowed to Park?
No

Approximate Parking Permit Cost: $20 per term

Dartmouth Parking Services:

(603) 646-2204
Robin.Guay@dartmouth.edu
http://www.dartmouth.edu/~parking

Parking Permits:

Permits are plentiful for upperclassmen, but parking near the center of campus is impossible for undergraduates to obtain.

→

Best Places to Find a Parking Spot:
Greek House

Good Luck Getting a Parking Spot Here:
Main Street

Common Parking Tickets:
Expired Meter: Enforced by Hanover Police
No Parking Zone: $50
Handicapped Zone: $50
Fire Lane: $50
Failure to Register: $50

Students Speak Out On...
Parking

{ **"Students have to park in A-Lot, which is about a ten minute walk from campus. During the weekends, though, you can park on campus without getting a ticket."**

Q **"Students mostly park in A-Lot,** the student parking lot. Beyond that, parking is very difficult. Hanover is extremely vigilant about checking meters and giving tickets to offenders, and the metered spots are only good for two hours, so parking is no picnic."

Q "Unless you're in a house or negotiate to park at one, forget about it**. A-Lot is a mile away from the far end of campus,** and cars get plowed in under snowdrifts. Guessing which one's yours isn't an easy task."

Q "It exists, somewhere beyond the third star on the left and straight on till morning. Seriously, though, I don't have a car and don't concern myself with parking. **Most students don't have cars."**

Q **"Freshmen can't have cars on campus,** but there are plenty of lots/permits available for upperclassmen. The lots aren't terribly close to the center of campus, but they aren't inconvenient."

Q "Freshmen can't have cars. **There isn't a lot of parking,** and it's mostly restricted to lots that are pretty far from the dorms."

Q "**Parking sucks.** It's hard to park, and the student lot is kind of far. If you're in a fraternity or sorority, you're lucky because you'll likely have a spot at the house, but otherwise it sucks. Since there is no crime, Hanover police give out parking tickets everyday, but honestly, you don't need a car there at all, the campus is relatively small."

Q "You can't have a car during your first year, and **you can apply for parking during your second year.**"

Q "Don't even think about it, freshmen. **A-Lot is out of the way,** but off campus/Greek housing has some parking for upperclassmen."

Q "It's basically a non-issue. **Almost everyone walks or bikes,** and those who need parking spaces can either purchase them from the College for a modest fee or arrange to use a fraternity parking space."

Q "**It sucks.** There is a place called 'A-Lot' where you are supposed to park but it is far away. You may find a spot elsewhere on campus, such as a frat lot, but expect to get many college parking tickets. Everyone does. It's strict and you cannot graduate without paying them. I think they are a little easier to beat than Hanover parking tickets, though."

Q "**There are few frats with extra spots** that rent them out, even to freshmen. However, watch out, because S&S will lock your wheel with a boot if you get enough tickets."

Q "There's **no indoor parking** except for a small lot in town, and every car I know of stopped working at least once during the year."

The College Prowler Take On...
Parking

Freshman can't have cars on campus, so keep that '91 Geo Prism at home. While spaces are available for upperclassmen, a good portion keeps their vehicles at home. A-Lot and other official parking is far off the beaten path, and don't even think of parking that car outside your dorm. S&S and H-Po are hyper-vigilant about tickets and will nail cars left unattended for a few minutes or on the street overnight.

Parking is surprisingly scarce for a school located in as small a location as Hanover. While students can comfortably walk anywhere on campus, the plethora of tickets is annoying, not to mention a waste of perfectly good paper. The best bet for a spot is Greek houses with lots, where even freshman can land a spot for the right price. Perhaps it's better that many students choose not to bring cars, however, as the New Hampshire will destroy your vehicle.

The College Prowler™ Grade on

Parking: C-

A high grade in this section indicates that parking is both available and affordable, and that parking enforcement isn't overly severe.

Transportation

The Lowdown On...
Transportation

Ways to Get Around Town

On Campus
Walk or Bike

Public Transportation
Advance Transit:
(802) 295-1824;
www.advancetranit.com

Taxi Cabs
Apex Car Service:
(603) 252-8294
Big Yellow Taxi: (603) 643-8294
Upper Valley Taxi: (802) 295-9455

Car Rentals
Avis, local: (603) 298-7753;
national: (800) 831-2847,
www.avis.com
Enterprise, local: (603) 298-0218; national: (800) 736-8222,
www.enterprise.com
Hertz, local: (603) 448-0634;
national: (800) 654-3131,
www.hertz.com
National, local: (603) 298-5701;
national: (800) 227-7368,
www.nationalcar.com
Rent-A-Wreck, local: (603) 448-6930; national: (800) 944-7501,
www.rentawreck.com
Thrifty, local: (802) 295-6611;
national: (800) 847-4389,
www.thrifty.com

Best Ways to Get Around Town:
Hitch a ride, though biking is often faster than driving within town.

Ways to Get Out of Town:

Airport:
Manchester Airport
(603) 624-6539
Manchester Airport is approximately 1.5 hours driving time from Hanover.

Airlines Serving Manchester:
Continental, (800) 523-3273, www.continental.com
Delta, (800) 221-1212, www.delta-air.com
Northwest, (800) 225-2525, www.nwa.com
Southwest, (800) 435-9792, www.southwest.com
United, (800) 241-6522, www.united.com
US Airways, (800) 428-4322, www.usairways.com

How to Get There:
Vermont Transit (see below)

A Bus Ride to the Airport Costs:
$20

Airport:
Logan Airport
(800) 23-LOGAN
Logan Airport is approximately 2.5 hours driving time from Hanover.

Airlines Serving Boston:
America West, (800) 235-9292, www.americawest.com
American, (800) 433-7300, www.aa.com
Continental, (800) 523-3273, www.continental.com
Delta, (800) 221-1212, www.delta-air.com
Northwest, (800) 225-2525, www.nwa.com
Southwest, (800) 435-9792, www.southwest.com
United, (800) 241-6522, www.united.com
US Airways, (800) 428-4322, www.usairways.com

How to Get There:
Dartmouth Coach, (800) 637-0123
A Dartmouth Coach departs from the Hanover Inn approximately every two hours. Coaches are comfortable and provide on-board movies.

A Bus Ride to the Airport Costs:
$35

Airport:
Lebanon Municipal Airport
(603) 298-8878
Lebanon Airport is approximately fifteen minutes from Hanover.

Airlines Serving Lebanon:
US Airways, (800) 428-4322, www.usairways.com

How to Get There:
Taxi (see above)

A Cab Ride to the Airport Costs:
$15

Greyhound, (800) 229-9424
Most Greyhound routes are operated by Vermont Transit, which can be reached at (800) 451-3292. Buses depart throughout the day from in front of the Hanover Inn, including multiple times per day for the Manchester Airport.

Amtrak, (800) USA-RAIL
Located across the Connecticut River in White River Junction, VT, The Amtrak station is less than five miles from campus. Trains one once daily between Montreal and New York's Penn Station, where trains to other destinations can be boarded.

Travel Agents
Anne Rose Travel,
25 Lebanon Street, Hanover, (603) 643-4100

Students Speak Out On...
Transportation

"There isn't any. It's not necessary. There is public transportation that takes you into town, but by the time you need to get there, you'll have friends with cars and won't need it. On campus, everything is in walking distance. If you need to go somewhere at night that's across campus, Safety and Security will drive you."

Q "**There's free transportation** (The college pays to let Dartmouth students use it for free) to West Lebanon but it takes six times as long as it would by a normal car."

Q "**Free local buses are great and easy to use**, though most people don't take advantage of them. Riding the bus to Boston can be expensive, but Dartmouth Coach is comfortable."

Q "Dartmouth Coach to Boston is mainly for the airport and kind of expensive as well. **Make friends with people who have cars** for those trips to Wal-Mart in West Leb."

Q "Leaving Hanover can be easy or hard, depending on where you want to go. Without a car, it's almost easier to escape on the Vermont Transit bus to Boston or Montreal for the weekend than it is to go to the Wal-Mart ten minutes away. **Getting to and from school can be a little tricky,** but Hanover is serviced by two major interstate— Routes 91 and 89—and cheap flights can be had into Manchester Airport. The regular bus service between Manchester and Hanover is a godsend."

Q **"There are a few buses out of Hanover every day.** They go to Burlington, Boston, New York, etc. It's pretty convenient, considering how isolated Hanover is."

Q **"There's bus transportation to local areas** as well as Boston, Montreal, New York, etc."

Q "For travel in the Hanover/West Lebanon area, **Advance Transit provides free bus shuttle services** to several local locations. Some upperclassmen have cars (despite their general uselessness), and those can be helpful for trips into Montreal, Boston, and New York."

Q "Well, it depends on where you're going. Manchester, Boston, or NYC, you're all set. Anywhere else, **good luck finding a cab.'"**

Q **"Public transportation is unnecessary,** since everything is so close. There are buses to Boston and there is a major train station the next town over."

Q "You don't really need it with a campus that small. **There's some sort of shuttle bus thing** that goes to West Lebanon (restaurants, other stores, etc) but just get a ride with a buddy. Lots of people have cars down there."

The College Prowler Take On...
Transportation

Students attest that the only subway in town serves sandwiches. An Amtrak train runs from nearby White River Junction. Greyhound-affiliate Vermont Transit buses service locations as near as the Dartmouth Skiway and as distant as New York or Montreal. Vermont Transit buses also run to Manchester Airport, while Dartmouth Coach goes to Boston's Logan Airport. While Lebanon Airport is just miles from campus, flights are few and very expensive. Local Advance Transit buses, while free to students, are unbearably slow. All buses depart from the Hanover Inn, just south of the Green.

Foot power is sufficient to get around campus, and, as isolated as Hanover is, it takes a long time to get anywhere. While easily accessible buses and trains make it easy to leave town, a bus ride and a couple of connecting flights make for a long day's travel when all you want is to sleep in your own bed. While local transportation exists, hitching a ride from a friend remains the best way to get around the area.

B-

The College Prowler™ Grade on

Transportation: B-

A high grade for Transportation indicates that campus buses, public buses, cabs, and rental cars are readily-available and affordable. Other determining factors include proximity to an airport and the necessity of transportation.

Weather

The Lowdown On...
Weather

Average Temperature

Fall: 59°F

Winter: 34°F

Spring: 65°F

Summer: 80°F

Average Precipitation

Fall: 3.4in.

Winter: 2.7in.

Spring: 3.6 in.

Summer: 3.45in

Students Speak Out On...
Weather

> "In the spring, summer, and fall, Dartmouth is a dream. But from December through mid-March, Hanover can get awfully cold. However, if you can take the snow, Hanover is beautiful in the winter."

Q **"It's cold**, but I happen to like it."

Q "**Get ready for cold, cold, cold winters.** The fall is pretty cool, winter is freezing and you can't see the ground at all, spring is pretty nice, and summer is beautiful."

Q "Personally, **I love the climate** of Hanover. Don't expect to wear shorts from October through the end of April, and don't be surprised to see snowflakes in the air from November through April."

Q "It's New England, so **the weather can be warm one day and freezing the next,** or sometimes go from hot to cold within 20 minutes, but I like it. The winter wasn't too bad this year (I'm from Boston so I'm used to it) but it is certainly an adjustment for Californians."

Q "**There is a huge spectrum of weather conditions** in Hanover, and I think that's one of the best attributes of Dartmouth. Every term feels completely new and different, in part because of the weather changes. With the D-Plan, you can see which seasons you like best and go from there. I personally love winter, and nothing beats a beautiful snowy day in Hanover."

Q "The fall weather is beautiful in Hanover, but **the winters are pretty gray** and the days are extremely short, so it can get depressing if you lock yourself up inside. If you get outside and ski or do whatever, the winter can be amazing (winter term was is my favorite)."

Q "**Don't come if you don't like cold weather and snow.** Do come if you like skiing—some of the best on the East Coast is minutes from campus. Hanover weather can be fickle, though. It reached as low as twenty-five below my freshman winter."

Q "**Last year the coldest it got was -15 degrees.** The spring can be cold and rainy/snowy, or it can be sunny and warm. It all depends on the year."

Q "Frigid in winter. Lots of snow. **The summer was really cool** too; it was about 40 degrees at night. But it's nice in the fall and spring, and I've heard that it varies from year to year too."

Q "The only real downside is the weather—**it sucks.** It rains a lot in the spring, it's hot in the summer and its damn cold in the winter, and there is always tons and tons of snow."

Q "It rains a lot and is often wet and gray. **When it's sunny, it's beautiful.** Enjoy it."

Q "New England weather changes all the time. You'll freeze your ass off in the winter but **the campus looks beautiful year round.**"

Q "We just had the worst winter in a century. Now is the time to come to Dartmouth; **we're due for some mild winters!**"

The College Prowler Take On...
Weather

Now's the time to buy a winter coat or three, because there's no escaping Hanover's icy cold winters Last winter was particularly frigid. With snow whitening the ground from Thanksgiving through Spring Break, you just may forget how the Green got its name. Mud season supplants winter when the snow finally melts but soon gives way to a beautiful and much-awaited spring. The fall is mild with gorgeous colors, while summer weather is idyllic.

Dartmouth is extremely scenic in all seasons. Some students construct their D-plans to avoid being on campus during the winter, while others go skiing to distract themselves from the cold. While six months of freezing temperatures are unpleasant, there'd be no Winter Carnival without them.

The College Prowler™ Grade on
Weather: C

A high Weather grade designates that temperatures are mild and rarely reach extremes, that the campus tends to be sunny rather than rainy, and that weather is fairly consistent rather than unpredictable.

Report Card Summary

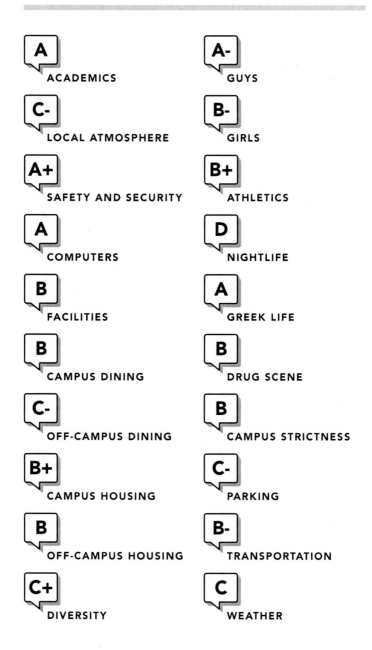

A
ACADEMICS

A-
GUYS

C-
LOCAL ATMOSPHERE

B-
GIRLS

A+
SAFETY AND SECURITY

B+
ATHLETICS

A
COMPUTERS

D
NIGHTLIFE

B
FACILITIES

A
GREEK LIFE

B
CAMPUS DINING

B
DRUG SCENE

C-
OFF-CAMPUS DINING

B
CAMPUS STRICTNESS

B+
CAMPUS HOUSING

C-
PARKING

B
OFF-CAMPUS HOUSING

B-
TRANSPORTATION

C+
DIVERSITY

C
WEATHER

Overall Experience

Students Speak Out On...
Overall Experience

> "I love Dartmouth! I've seen so many schools, and I can't think of a single substantial change I would like to see on our campus that any other school has. Of course, Dartmouth isn't perfect for everyone, but I guarantee that if you do decide to come, you'll enjoy the four years you have here and probably look back wishing they didn't go by so quickly."

Q "That's a tough one . . . I'd say that I'm enjoying Dartmouth and **I love my friends there.** As far as the location, I don't really like it all that much, but I do feel really safe at Dartmouth and it's nice to be away from a city for a while."

Q "Most college students like their colleges. **Dartmouth students are often in love with their school.** My personal passion for Dartmouth has exceeded my own expectations, and I have found myself enormously happy at Dartmouth, despite initial misgivings. The people, resources, and general campus activity have made my Dartmouth experience so far entirely successful, and I am utterly content at Dartmouth. I can't wait for my summer to end so I can get back!"

Q "My time so far at Dartmouth has been absolutely wonderful. **It'd be hard to imagine a better college experience.** The scenery is beautiful, everybody has fun, and the students are all above average. Sometimes the place seems very similar to a summer camp."

Q **"Academically, I think I've learned a lot at Dartmouth.** I went on their Foreign Study Program in Paris last winter and that was amazing. I think that the professors are all really nice and really intelligent and Dartmouth is definitely a 'giant' step up from high school."

Q "If you want to find out a little more about campus life, you can go to www.thedartmouth.com. **The school newspaper is pretty helpful** with assessing what life is like and how important frats are, etc."

Q "I love Dartmouth with a passion. **It's an absolutely incredible place.** I definitely picked the right school."

Q **"The school honestly cares about the students' social lives**. The Dartmouth Outing Club program helped me meet a bunch of nice kids before school ever started. Then, from the moment I left the woods, they have been planning activities for us."

Q "You can't walk out your door **without being invited to go somewhere,** play some sport, or eat."

Q **"It's a great place to go to school**, and I like it a lot."

Q "It's really an incredible place. But its nothing like the city, **it's a very rural campus."**

Q "Dartmouth was the time of my life. **Academics were spectacular,** and the social life was a blast. Greek life was definitely a large part of the social scene, but I was in a house and loved every minute of it, lots of solid extra-curricular activities."

Q "**I felt the campus was very safe.** People were incredibly friendly. The dining hall food was pretty good compared to most other colleges, but after I moved off campus (when I finally had some money), I ate out a lot because the local restaurants were great."

Q "It is great, **just nothing like New York.** It's way out in the sticks and not urban. However, the campus is very nice and has plenty of buildings. The many activities you can get involved in will keep you busy. The administration tries to bring in some good concerts and stuff each term."

Q "**After four years I was ready to leave,** but I thoroughly enjoyed my time there. I can't imagine fitting in better or having a grander time anywhere else."

Q "It is a good experience and the people there are mostly friendly. **I didn't pay too much attention to social stuff** while I was there, just hung out with my buddies and joined a frat. As a school it's very good for government, economics, computer science, psychology, and cognitive science."

The College Prowler Take On...
Overall Experience

According to numerous surveys, Dartmouth students are among the happiest in the land. And with a gorgeous campus, great food, spacious dorms, and a vibrant party scene, why shouldn't they be? There are certainly a host of minor drawbacks to attending school in Hanover —isolation, no parking, and no more rope swing. However, unique positives like the study abroad program, top-notch academics, and numerous outdoor opportunities blow these negatives out of the water for most students.

Dartmouth students have perhaps the strongest love for their school of any college kids in the country. Such passion is what motivates alums to trek to Hanover for big weekends and party like teenagers, long after their heyday has passed. Dartmouth is a friendly, pleasant place, providing the vast majority of its students with a genuine Ivy League experiences on top of the big diploma.

The Inside Scoop

The Lowdown On...
The Inside Scoop

Dartmouth Slang

Know the slang, know the school. The following is a list of things you really need to know before coming to Dartmouth. The more of these words you know, the better off you'll be.

AT: Appalachian Trail; runs through campus.

Banner Student: Online website containing personal academic information.

Blackboard: Online service where professors post course material.

Blitz: E-mail; can be used as any part of speech.

CD: Community director; no one's sure what they do, except boss around the UGAs.

Coco: College Courses, interdisciplinary in nature.

D, The: Student newspaper; the nation's oldest and, many allege, worst.

Dartmouth Review, The: Independent conservative student newspaper.

DA$H: An account used for on-campus, non-food purchases; it's not real money.

➡

Dick's House: Student health center.

Direct Connect: System for exchanging music and movies.

EBAs: Everything But Anchovies; they deliver until 2 a.m.

FO&M: Facilities Operations and Management.

Free Press, The: Liberal, school-supported newspaper.

FSP: Foreign study program.

Green, The: Huge grassy rectangle at the center of campus.

HB: Hinman Box, where you pick up your mail; located in the Hop.

H-Po: Hanover Police; REALLY avoid when drunk.

Hop, The: Hopkins Center; performing arts center of campus.

HTH: Hometown honey, with whom you will break up shortly after arriving on campus.

LSA: Language Study Abroad.

NRO: Non-recording option; when invoked, allows you to receive an 'NR' if you fail to achieve a desired grade in a class.

ORL: Office of Residential Life.

Parkhursted: Suspended; named after the administration building, Parkhurst.

Pong: Beer pong; played exclusively with handle-less paddles

PUBLIC: Name of network for Apple users.

Robo: Robinson Hall; home of the Dartmouth Outing Club and other student organizations.

Rocky: Rockefeller Center; government center.

Senior Fence: Surrounds part of the green; don't sit on it if you're not a senior.

'Shmenu: The Green Book; contains pictures of all the freshman.

'Shmob: The large group in which most freshman travel.

Sketchy: All-purpose word to describe anyone or anything about which you are skeptical; use liberally.

SA Cash: Debit account that can be used in town.

Sphinx: Large, tomblike home to a secret society, located in the middle of campus.

S&S: Safety and security; avoid when drunk.

Term: Used most often in place of 'quarter'; saying 'semester' will give you away as a newbie in a heartbeat.

Thayer: Dining hall and engineering school. Pay attention to context clues.

Tree Houses: Hastily constructed and undesirable dwellings near the river.

Tripee: Fellow member of your Freshman trip.

UGA: Undergraduate assistant; a supposedly less mean version of RA.

Webster Ave: Fraternity (and sorority) row.

WILSON: Name of network for PC users.

Things I Wish I Knew Before Coming to Dartmouth

That orientation is by far the best time to meet people…and go to Frat Row.

That all that time I procrastinated could have been spent having fun.

That I only have time for two or three extracurricular activities.

How few nice clothes I need and how many crazy clothes I could use.

That the Choates were nothing to worry about.

How cold a New Hampshire winter really is.

How to ski…or camp.

Tips to Succeed at Dartmouth

Always go to class when midterms or finals are coming up

Take naps in the afternoon

Have at least one good friend in every class

Use distributive requirements to take fun classes

Avoid morning classes or Tuesday/Thursday classes alltogether

Plan a break or fun extracurricular activity into your schedule

Find two or three good study spots and move around

Don't let BlitzMail consume your life

Dartmouth Urban Legends

• Any American Indian admitted will receive full a scholarship to Dartmouth. (While this is untrue, Dartmouth has renewed its original commitment to Native Americans and now has more American Indian students than the other Ivies combined.)

• Students caught drinking during orientation and before matriculation will have their admission rescinded.

• Playboy once ranked Dartmouth's guys the second-hottest in the country.

• Beer pong was invented at Dartmouth; students believe their paddle version is a purer game than the oft-played Beirut.

School Spirit

Love for the College on the Hill extends far beyond the Dartmouth jock-wear most students are perpetually sporting. From Freshman Trips forward, Dartmouth students are imbued with a fierce love of their unique and historic institution. The College's small size fosters a single Dartmouth community, and students often make the trek to Hanover during their off terms. Dartmouth alumni are fiercely loyal and noted for being generous with pocketbooks and connections. However, there is a sense among even recent graduates that the school is being slowly transformed into a cookie-cutter research institution. For now at least, Hanover is filled with students who love their school and are sublimely happy.

Traditions

Homecoming
Each term has one "big" (read: party) weekend, and in Fall, the chief celebration is Homecoming. Freshmen are the focus of the weekend, as they are officially welcomed into the Dartmouth family. On Friday night, upperclassmen collect all the pea-greens during a Freshman Sweep. Everyone marches en masse to the center of the Green, where a giant bonfire ensues. Freshmen run around it one hundred times plus the last two digits of their class year while older students and alumni egg them on.

Winter Carnival

Back before Dartmouth was coeducation, the long winter was warmed on this weekend as hundreds of women were bused in from all over the country. A variety of sporting contests are held, and brave souls leap into Occom Pond to partake in the Polar Bear Jump. Dormitories and Greek houses erect small snow sculptures on their property, while a giant sculpture is carved at the center of the Green.

Green Key

With temperatures finally mild, Dartmouth students take to the great outdoors to celebrate. Green Key is arguably the biggest party weekend of the year as students bask in the sun for three or four straight days. Barbeques and concerts abound, with some fraternities throwing annual parties.

Tubestock

Another 3-4 day round of carousing culminates when the thousand or so students on campus don their bathing suits and head to the Connecticut River, where they float themselves and large quantities of beer on homemade rafts and inner tubes.

Sophomore Summer

Summer school sounds less than glamorous, but it means three months of fantastic weather and class bonding each sophomore class. Students often take only two courses while lounging the summer away at "Camp Dartmouth."

Lone Pine

When establishing the school on a hill, Dartmouth founder Eleazar Wheelock noticed one crooked pine tree among a cluster of straight ones. This he took to be a symbol of the College, which would struggle to survive through its own literal and metaphorical winters. While the Lone Pine has since been struck by lightning, Bartlett Tower stands in tribute to its memory, and its glazed stump is preserved.

Daniel Webster

When a disgruntled trustee colluded with the New Hampshire governor to make Dartmouth a public university, the College was represented by its most famous alumnus. The great statesman argued for Dartmouth before the United States Supreme Court, which subsequently allowed the institution to remain private. Webster concluded his plea with remarks that are still echoed by students to this day: "This is, as I have said sir, a small college... and yet there are those who love it."

Ledyard Challenge

Before graduation, students are supposed to swim naked across the Connecticut River to Vermont (where nudity is legal), and then scamper in the buff back across the Ledyard Bridge.

Indian

Dartmouth was originally founded for the education of Native Americans, and Indians became embedded in College lore. The College failed to follow through on their original charter, with fewer then 20 Native Americans graduating before the 1960s, but in the last few decades Dartmouth has built one of the strongest Native American Studies programs in the country. While the school has never had an "official mascot," the Indian-head logo graced The Dartmouth masthead, as well as athletes, for decades. Since the Indian was banned in 1974, the Clay Pipe Ceremony has been canceled, while only a few seniors carry Indian-head canes at graduation. Recent efforts to replace the nebulous "Big Green" moniker with a moose have failed.

Finding a Job or Internship

The Lowdown On...
Finding a Job or Internship

If your connections via Uncle Harold fail—or should you need some—seek out Career Services, which has a generally positive reputation around campus and provides comprehensive career help. Each fall, dozens of companies trek up to Dartmouth to woo Seniors during Corporate Recruiting.

Advice

Career Services can be of help from the first summer onward, so attending a first-time users session immediately after arriving on campus can be especially helpful. Always keep a resume on file and monitor the Career Services BlitzMail Bulletin for interesting opportunities. Also, students interested in government should seek out the resources of the Rockefeller Center, which has a number of specific listings and internships.

Career Center Resources & Services

•Job/Internship Search Workshops

•Job and Internship Listings (MonterTRAK)

•On-Campus Recruiting

•Blitz Bulletin

•Graduate Advising

•Electronic Portfolio

Firms That Most Frequently Hire Graduates:

Goldman Sachs, Dartmouth College, Lehman Brothers, JP Morgan, UBS Payne Webber, Teach for America, Morgan Stanley/Dean Witter, Bain and Company, Soloman Smith Barney.

Alumni

The Lowdown On...
Alumni

Website:
http://www.dartmouth.edu/
alumni

Office:
6068 Blunt Alumni Center
Hanover, NH 03755
(888) 228-6068
alumni.relations@dartmouth.
edu

Services Available
Online directory, e-mail
account

Blunt Alumni Center:
Blunt is located just northwest
of the Green and often
hosts alumni in a tent on big
weekends.

Major Alumni Events

The three regular-year party weekends —Homecoming, Winter Carnvial, and Green Key—bring a multitude of alums back to Hanover. Additionally, class reunions are held every five years the week after commencement. Turnout for these reunions is very high, and the events raise a great deal of money for Dartmouth.

Alumni Publications

Dartmouth Alumni Magazine

(603) 646-2256

Alumni.Maganize@dartmouth.edu

Did You Know?

- **Daniel Webster** (Class of 1801), Secretary of State under three Presidents
- **Robert Frost** (Class of 1896), Pulitzer Prize-winning poet
- **Theodore ("Dr.") Seuss Geisel** (Class of '25), World-famous children's author
- **Nelson Rockefeller** (Class of '30), Vice-President under Gerald Ford.
- **Dr. C. Everett Koop** (Class of '37), U.S. Surgeon General under President Reagan
- **(Mister) Fred Rogers** (Class of '50), Children's television entertainer
- **H. Carl McCall** (Class of '58), Former New York comptroller and gubernatorial candidate
- **Louis Gerstner** (Class of '63), Former IBM CEO
- **Paavo Lipponen** (Class of '64), Former Finnish Prime Minister
- **Robert Reich** (Class of '68), U.S. Secretary of Labor under President Clinton
- **Paul Gigot** (Class of '77), Pulitzer Prize-winning journalist
- **Dinesh D'Souza** (Class of '83), Political journalist and cultural critic
- **Jay Fiedler** (Class of '94), Miami Dolphins quarterback

Student Organizations

There are more than 400 student organizations on campus. See *http://www.dartmouth.edu/~sao/coso/orgs.html* for organization website. The following is a partial list:

Academic Competition Groups

College Bowl

Mock Trial Society

Model United Nations

Parliamentary Debate Team

Dartmouth Ethics Society

Culture Specific Groups

AfriCaSO

Club Singapura

Dartmouth Asian Organization (DAO)

Dartmouth Chinese Culture Society

Dartmouth Rainbow Alliance (DRA)

Eastern European Cultural Society

Hokupa'a

German Club

International Students Association (I.S.A.)

Irish Society

Italian Club

Japan Society

Korean American Students Association (KASA)

La Alianza Latina

M.E.Ch.A. (Movimiento Estudiantil Chicano/a de Aztlan)

Milan

MOSAIC

Native Americans at Dartmouth (NAD)

Russian Club

Shamis

Vietnamese Student Association

Honor Societies

Society of Collegiate Scholars (NSCS)

Issue Oriented Groups

Coalition Against Abusive Relationships Everywhere (C.A.R.E.)

Coalition for Life

College Republicans

Dartmouth College Greens

Dartmouth Israel Public Awareness Committee (DIPAC)

Dartmouth Students for Reproductive Rights

Dartmouth Vegetarian Alliance

Gay Straight Alliance

Independent Forum

Ivy Council at Dartmouth

Libertarians at Dartmouth

Occum's Razors

Senior Symposium

Student Global AIDS Network

Voces Clamantium

Women of Color Collective

Young Democrats

Performing Groups

Aires

Ballet Folklorico de Dartmouth

Casual Thursday

Chinese Dance Troupe

Cords, The

Dartmouth Brass Society

Dartmouth Chamber Orchestra

Dartmouth Flute Choir

Dartmouth Soul Society

Dartmouth Steel

Decibelles

Displaced Theater Company

Dodecaphonics

Dog Day Players

Far Off Broadway Productions

Final Cut

FUSION

Jump Start

Liquid Theory Dance Performance Group

Rockapellas

SHEBA

Subtleties

Vandana

Wordthieves

X.ado

Pre-Professional Groups

AISES

Club of Dartmouth Entrepreneurs

Dartmouth Chemistry Society

Nathan Smith Premedical Society

Pre-Veterinary Medicine Society

Society of Women Engineers

Publication/Media Groups

Aegis

Aporia, part of Occum's Razors

AREA

Dartmouth Contemporary, The

DTV

Free Press

History and Classics Journal

IMAGO Media

Jack-O-Lantern

Main Street

Stonefence Review

The Green Magazine

The Tradition

Word Magazine

Recreational Groups

Asgard

Bridge Club

Chess Club

Creative Gaming

Dartmouth Association of Culinary Arts (DACA)

Dartmouth Citrus Alliance

Harlequins

Medieval Enthusiasts at Dartmouth

Photography Club

Swing Kids

Thursday Night Salsa

Tolkein Society

The Best & The Worst

The Ten BEST Things About Dartmouth:

1	Tight-knit community
2	Beer Pong
3	The D-Plan
4	Wireless
5	Outdoor opportunities
6	Big weekends
7	Three classes
8	Friendly professors
9	The Green on a beautiful day
10	EBAs at 2:15 a.m.

The Ten **WORST** Things About Dartmouth:

1 Dark winter days

2 Isolation

3 The D-Plan

4 Wrangling over diversity

5 Parking

6 Fines

7 Hanover Nightlife

8 Kresge Fitness Center on a crowded afternoon

9 Student apathy

10 Administration crackdown on the Greeks

Visiting Dartmouth College

The Lowdown On...
Visiting

Hotel Information

1830 Shire Town Inn
Woodstock, VT
Phone: (802) 457-1830
Distance/Time to Campus: 30 min.

Adairs Motor Inn
Danbury, NH
Phone: (603) 768-9872
Distance/Time to Campus: 45 min.

Airport Economy Inn
West Lebanon, NH
Phone: (603) 298-8888
Distance/Time to Campus: 7 miles/10 min

Alden Country Inn
Lyme, NH
Phone: (800) 794-2296
Distance/Time to Campus: 20 min

Ardmore Inn
Woodstock, VT
Phone: (802) 457-3887
Distance/Time to Campus: 30 min

Bed & Breakfast of Bank Street
Lebanon, NH
Phone: (603) 448-2041
Distance/Time to Campus: 15 min

➔

Best Western at the Junction
White River Junction, VT
Phone: (802) 295-3015
Distance/Time to Campus: 15 min

Best Western Sunapee
Lake Sunapee, NH
Phone: (800) 528-1234
Distance/Time to Campus: 30 min

Bradford Motel
Bradford, VT
Phone: (802) 222-4467
Distance/Time to Campus: 20 miles

Breakfast on the Connecticut
Lyme, NH
Phone: (603) 353-4444
Distance/Time to Campus: 12 miles/ 20 min

Burkhaven Motel
Sunapee, NH
Phone: (800) 567-2788
Distance/Time to Campus: 30 min

Carriage House of Woodstock
Woodstock, VT
Phone: (802) 457-4322
Distance/Time to Campus: 30 min

Chieftain Motor Inn
Hanover, NH
Phone: (603) 643-2550
Distance/Time to Campus: 2.5 miles

Coach an Four Motel
White River Junction, VT
Phone: (802) 295-2210
Distance/Time to Campus: 4.5 miles/ 15 min

Colonial Farm Inn
New London, NH
Phone: (603) 526-6121
Distance/Time to Campus: 30 miles/ 35 min

Columns Motor Lodge
Sharon, VT
Phone: (802) 763-7040
Distance/Time to Campus: 20 min

Comfort Inn
White River Junction, VT
toll free: 800-628-7727
Phone: (802) 295-3051
Distance/Time to Campus: 10 min

Coolidge Hotel
White River Junction, VT
Phone: (802) 295-3118
Distance/Time to Campus: 5 miles/ 10 min

Days Inn/Holiday Inn Express
Lebanon, NH
Phone: (603) 448-5070
Distance/Time to Campus: 3miles/ 5-10 min

Deer Brook Inn
Woodstock, VT
Phone: (802) 672-3713
Distance/Time to Campus: 30 min

Dowds Country Inn
Lyme, NH
Phone: (603) 795-4712
Distance/Time to Campus: 10 miles/ 10 min

Fairlee Motel
Fairlee, VT
Phone: (802) 333-9192
Distance/Time to Campus: 8 min

Fairway
New London, NH
Phone: (603) 526-6040
Distance/Time to Campus: 30 min

Fireside Inn
West Lebanon, NH
Phone: (603) 298-5906
Distance/Time to Campus: 10 min

Gibson House Gallery and Bed & Breakfast
Haverhill, NH
Phone: (603) 989-3125
Distance/Time to Campus: 25 min

Goddard Mansion Bed & Breakfast
Claremont, NH
Phone: (603) 543-0603
Distance/Time to Campus: 30 min

Half-Acre Motel
Sharon, VT
Phone: (802) 763-8010
Distance/Time to Campus: 25 miles/ 15-20 min

Hampton Inn
White River Junction, VT
Phone: (802) 296-2800
Distance/Time to Campus: 15 min

Hanover Inn
Hanover, NH
Phone: (603) 643-4300
Distance/Time to Campus: On Campus

Hilltop Motel
Newport, NH
Phone: (603) 863-3456
Distance/Time to Campus: 35 min

Home Hill French Inn and Restaurant
Plainfield, NH
Phone: (603) 675-6165
Distance/Time to Campus: 20 min

Inn at Ragged Edge Farm
Wilmot, NH
Phone: (603) 735-6484
Distance/Time to Campus: 45 min

Jackson House Inn
Woodstock, VT
Phone: (802) 457-2065
Distance/Time to Campus: 30 min

Juniper Hill Inn
Windsor, VT
Phone: (802) 674-5273
Distance/Time to Campus: 20 min

Lake Morey Resort
Fairlee, VT
Phone: (802) 457-3312
Distance/Time to Campus: 15-20 min

Lamplighter
New London, NH
Phone: (603) 526-6484
Distance/Time to Campus: 25-30 min

Lincoln Inn
Woodstock, VT
Phone: (802) 457-3312
Distance/Time to Campus: 30 min

Mary Keane House
Enfield, NH
Phone: (603) 632-4241
Distance/Time to Campus: 12 miles/ 15-20 min

New London Inn
New London, NH
Phone: (603) 526-2791
Distance/Time to Campus:
30-45 min

Newport Motel
Newport, NH
Phone: (603) 863-1440
Distance/Time to Campus: 35
miles

Norwich Inn
Norwich, VT
Phone: (802) 649-1143
Distance/Time to Campus: 2
miles

October Country Inn
Bridgewater Corners, VT
Phone: (802) 572-3412
Distance/Time to Campus: 25
min

Ottauquechee Motor Lodge
Woodstock, VT
Phone: (802) 672-3404
Distance/Time to Campus: 35
min

Parker House Inn
Quechee, VT
Phone: (802) 295-6077
Distance/Time to Campus: 15
min

Pierces Inn
Etna, NH
Phone: (603) 643-2997
Distance/Time to Campus: 5.5
miles/ 12 min

Piermont Inn Old Church
Piermont, NH
Phone: (603) 272-4820
Distance/Time to Campus: 30
min

Pine Crest Motel
White River Junction, VT
Phone: (802) 295-2725
Distance/Time to Campus: 10
miles/ 10-15 min

Pleasant View Motel
White River Junction, VT
Phone: (802) 295-3485
Distance/Time to Campus: 5
miles

**Quality Inn at Quechee
Gorge**
Quechee, VT
Phone: (802) 295 7600
Distance/Time to Campus: 15
min

**Quechee Inn at Marshland
Farm**
Quechee, VT
Phone: (802) 295-3133
10-12 min

Ramada Inn
White River Junction, VT
Phone: (802) 295-3000
Distance/Time to Campus: 5
miles/ 10 min

Residence Inn by Marriott
Lebanon, NH
Phone: (603) 643-4511
Distance/Time to Campus: 5
min

Shady Lawn Motel
White River Junction, VT
Phone: (802) 295-7118
Distance/Time to Campus: 15
min

Shire Motel
46 Woodstock, VT
Phone: (802) 457-2211
Distance/Time to Campus:

Silver Maple Lodge & Cottages
Fairlee, VT
Phone: (800) 666-1946
Distance/Time to Campus: 17 miles/ 20 min

Sunset Motor Inn
Lebanon, NH
Phone: (603) 298-8721
Distance/Time to Campus: 5 min

Super 8 Motel
White River Junction, VT
Phone: (802) 295-7577
Distance/Time to Campus: 15 min

The Woodbridge Inn of Woodstock
Woodstock, VT
Phone: (802) 672-1800
Distance/Time to Campus: 30-35 min

Three Church Street
Woodstock, VT
Phone: (802) 457-1925
Distance/Time to Campus: 30 min

Trumbull House B & B
Hanover, NH
Phone: (800) 651-5141
Distance/Time to Campus: 4 miles

Village Inn of Woodstock
Woodstock, VT
Phone: (802) 457-1255
30 min

Warren Village Inn, LLC
Warren, NH
Phone: (603) 764-5600
Distance/Time to Campus: 25 min

Woodbridge Inn
Bridgewater, VT
Phone: (802) 672-1800
Distance/Time to Campus: 20 min

Woodstock Inn & Resort
Woodstock, VT
Phone: (802) 457-1100
Distance/Time to Campus: 30 min

Woodstocker Bed & Breakfast
Woodstock, VT
Phone: (802) 457-3896
Distance/Time to Campus: 20-25 min

Take a Campus Virtual Tour
http://www.dartmouth.edu/~tour

To Schedule a Group Information Session or Interview

From January through mid-November, half hour group sessions are conducted at 10 a.m. Monday-Friday. Information sessions are also held at 10 a.m. and 11 a.m on Saturdays from mid-September through mid-November.

Campus Tours

Campus tours are conducted at various times throughout the year. During most of the fall, winter, and spring terms, they are given at 10 a.m. and 2 p.m. Monday-Friday and at 10 a.m and 12 p.m. on Saturday. Additional tours are conducted during summer term and peak times, while tours may be cut during off-peak times, including when school is not in session. Always call ahead to confirm tour times.

Interviews:

On-campus interviews are available to rising seniors from mid-June through mid-November. Please call the admissions office at least three weeks in advance of your visit to schedule an interview.

Overnight Visits:

Hosting is available for juniors in May and seniors in October and November. Students will stay with a current Dartmouth student on a Monday through Thursday night and must bring a sleeping bag and spending money. Please call the admissions office to schedule your stay.

Dimensions Weekend, which takes place every spring, invites all accepted students to stay at Dartmouth for a weekend. It is an incredible time, and almost every student who goes ends up matriculating at Dartmouth.

Directions to Campus

From the Boston area (~2.5 hours):

•Take I-93 north to I-89 north at Concord, N.H.

•Get off I-89 at Exit 18 in Lebanon, N.H. onto Route 120. (A sign says that it is the exit for Dartmouth College.)

•Bear right off the exit, heading north on Rt.120 into Hanover.

•4.1 miles from the exit, Rt. 120 forks at a traffic light.

•Bear right at the fork, following Rt. 120 one-half mile on South Park Street to the second traffic light.

•Turn left at the light, onto East Wheelock Street.

•Follow East Wheelock for two-tenths of a mile, when you will come to the Hopkins Center (left) and the Dartmouth Green (right).

From Burlington, Vt. (~1.5 hours):

•Take I-89 south to I-91 north in White River Junction, Vt. See following description.

From New York (~5 hours), southern New England and points south:

•Take I-91 north to exit 13 at Norwich, Vt.

•Bear right off the exit, across the Ledyard Bridge spanning the Connecticut River.

•Continue up the hill (West Wheelock Street) to the top of the hill and to the traffic light in the center of town - nine-tenths of a mile from the interstate exit.

•To your left at the light is the Dartmouth Green; to your right is the Hanover Inn.

Words to Know

Academic Probation – A student can receive this if they fail to keep up with their school's academic minimums. Those who are unable to improve their grades after receiving this warning can possibly face dismissal.

Beer Pong / Beirut – A drinking game with numerous cups of beer arranged in a particular pattern on each side of a table. The goal is to get a ping pong ball into one of the opponent's cups by throwing the ball or hitting it with a paddle. If the ball lands in a cup, the opponent is required to drink the beer.

Bid – An invitation from a fraternity or sorority to pledge their specific house.

Blue-Light Phone – Brightly-colored phone posts with a blue light bulb on top. These phones exist for security purposes and are located at various outside locations around most campuses. If a student has an emergency or is feeling endangered, they can pick up one of these phones (free of charge) to connect with campus police or an escort service.

Campus Police – Policemen who are specifically assigned to a given institution. Campus police are not regular city officers; they are employed by the university in a full-time capacity.

Club Sports – A level of sports that falls somewhere between varsity and intramural. If a student is unable to commit to a varsity team but has a lot of passion for athletics, a club sport could be a better, less intense option. If a club sport still requires too much commitment, intramurals often involve no traveling and a lot less time.

Cocaine – An illegal drug. Also known as "coke" or "blow," cocaine often resembles a white crystalline or powdery substance. It is highly addictive and dangerous.

Common Application – An application that students can use to apply to multiple schools.

Course Registration – The time when a student selects what courses they would like for the upcoming quarter or semester. Prior to registration, it is best to have an idea of several back-up courses in case a particular class becomes full. If a course is full, a student can place themselves on the waitlist, although this still does not guarantee entry.

Division Athletics – Athletics range from Division I to Division III. Division IA is the most competitive, while Division III is considered to be the least competitive.

Dorm – Short for dormitory, a dorm is an on-campus housing facility. Dorms can provide a range of options from suite-style rooms to more communal options that include shared bathrooms. Most first-year students live in dorms. Some upperclassmen who wish to stay on campus also choose this option.

Early Action – A way to apply to a school and get an early acceptance response without a binding commitment. This is a system that is becoming less and less available.

Early Decision – An option that students should use only if they are positive that a place is their dream school. If a student applies to a school using the early decision option and is admitted, they are required and bound to attend that university. Admission rates are usually higher with early decision students because the school knows that a student is making them their first choice.

Ecstasy – An illegal drug. Also known as "E" or "X," ecstasy looks like a pill and most resembles an aspirin. Considered a party drug, ecstasy is very dangerous and can be deadly.

Ethernet – An extremely fast internet connection that is usually available in most university-owned residence halls. To use an Ethernet connection properly, a student will need a network card and cable for their computer.

Fake ID – A counterfeit identification card that contains false information. Most commonly, students get fake IDs and change their birthdates so that they appear to be older than 21 (of legal drinking age). Even though it is illegal, many college students have fake IDs in hopes of purchasing alcohol or getting into bars.

Frosh – Slang for "freshmen."

Hazing – Initiation rituals that must be completed for membership into some fraternities or sororities. Numerous universities have outlawed hazing due to its degrading or dangerous requirements.

Sports (IMs) – A popular, and usually free, student activity where students create teams and compete against other groups for fun. These sports vary in competitiveness and can include a range of activities—everything from billiards to water polo. IM sports are a great way to meet people with similar interests.

Keg – Officially called a half barrel, a keg contains roughly 200 12-ounce servings of beer and is often found at college parties.

LSD – An illegal drug. Also known as acid, this hallucinogenic drug most commonly resembles a tab of paper.

Marijuana – An illegal drug. Also known as weed or pot; besides alcohol, marijuana is one of the most commonly-found drugs on campuses across the country.

Major –The focal point of a student's college studies; a specific topic that is studied for a degree. Examples of majors include physics, English, history, computer science, economics, business, and music. Many students decide on a specific major before arriving on campus, while others are simply "undecided" and figure it out later. Those who are extremely interested in two areas can also choose to double major.

Meal Block – The equivalent of one meal. Students on a "meal plan" usually receive a fixed number of meals per week.

Each meal, or "block," can be redeemed at the school's dining facilities in place of cash. More often than not, if a student fails to use their weekly allotment of meal blocks, they will be forfeited.

Minor – An additional focal point in a student's education. Often serving as a compliment or addition to a student's main area of focus, a minor has fewer requirements and prerequisites to fulfill than a major. Minors are not required for graduation from most schools; however some students who want to further explore many different interests choose to have both a major and a minor.

Mushrooms – An illegal drug. Also known as "shrooms," this drug looks like regular mushrooms but are extremely hallucinogenic.

Off-Campus Housing – Housing from a particular landlord or rental group that is not affiliated with the university. Depending on the college, off-campus housing can range from extremely popular to non-existent. Those students who choose to live off campus are typically given more freedom, but they also have to deal with things such as possible subletting scenarios, furniture, and bills. In addition to these factors, rental prices and distance often affect a student's decision to move off campus.

Office Hours – Time that teachers set aside for students who have questions about the coursework. Office hours are a good place for students to go over any problems and to show interest in the subject material.

Pledging – The time after a student has gone through rush, received a bid, and has chosen a particular fraternity or sorority they would like to join. Pledging usually lasts anywhere from one to two semesters. Once the pledging period is complete and a particular student has done everything that is required to become a member, they are considered a brother or sister. If a fraternity or a sorority would decide to "haze" a group of students, these initiation rituals would take place during the pledging period.

Private Institution – A school that does not use taxpayers dollars to help subsidize education costs. Private schools typically cost more than public schools and are usually smaller.

Prof – Slang for "professor."

Public Institution – A school that uses taxpayers dollars to help subsidize education costs. Public schools are often a good value for in-state residents and tend to be larger than most private colleges.

Quarter System (sometimes referred to as the Trimester System) – A type of academic calendar system. In this setup, students take classes for three academic periods. The first quarter usually starts in late September or early October and concludes right before Christmas. The second quarter usually starts around early to mid–January and finishes up around March or April. The last quarter, or "third quarter," usually starts in late March or early April and finishes up in late May or Mid-June. The fourth quarter is summer. The major difference between the quarter system and semester system is that students take more courses but with less coverage.

RA (Resident Assistant) – A student leader who is assigned to a particular floor in a dormitory in order to help to the other students who live there. A RA's duties include ensuring student safety and providing guidance or assistance wherever possible.

Recitation – An extension of a specific course; a "review" session of sorts. Because some classes are so large, recitations offer a setting with fewer students where students can ask questions and get help from professors or TAs in a more personalized environment. As a result, it is common for most large lecture classes to be supplemented with recitations.

Rolling Admissions – A form of admissions. Most commonly found at public institutions, schools with this type of policy continue to accept students throughout the year until their class sizes are met. For example, some schools begin accepting students as early as December and will continue to do so until April or May.

Room and Board – This is typically the combined cost of a university-owned room and a meal plan.

Room Draw/Housing Lottery – A common way to pick on-campus room assignments for the following year. If a student decides to remain in university-owned housing, they are assigned a unique number that, along with seniority, is used to choose their new rooms for the next year.

Rush – The period in which students can meet the brothers and sisters of a particular chapter and find out if a given fraternity or sorority is right for them. Rushing a fraternity or a sorority is not a requirement at any school. The goal of rush is to give students who are serious about pledging a feel for what to expect.

Semester System – The most common type of academic calendar system at college campuses. This setup typically includes two semesters in a given school year. The "fall" semester starts around the end of August or early September and finishes right before winter vacation. The "spring" semester usually starts in mid-January and ends around late April or May.

Student Center/Rec Center/Student Union – A common area on campus that often contains study areas, recreation facilities, and eateries. This building is often a good place to meet up with fellow students and is most commonly used as a hangout. Depending on the school, the student center can have a huge role or a non-existent role in campus life.

Student ID – A university-issued photo ID that serves as a student's key to many different functions within an institution. Some schools require students to show these cards in order to get into dorms, libraries, cafeterias, and other facilities. In addition to storing meal plan information, in some cases, a student ID can actually work as a debit card and allow students to purchase things from bookstores or local shops.

Suite – A type of dorm room. Unlike other places that have communal bathrooms that are shared by the entire floor, a suite has a private bathroom. Suite-style dorm rooms can house anywhere from two to ten students.

TA (Teacher's Assistant) – An undergraduate or grad student who helps in some manner with a specific course. In some cases, a TA will teach a class, assist a professor, grade assignments, or conduct office hours.

Undergraduate – A student who is in the process of studying for their Bachelor (college) degree.

ABOUT THE AUTHOR:

This book has given me the opportunity to fuse my passion for writing and the college search process. I deeply hope it has provided you with an insider's look at the college I have grown to love.

I am now a sophomore at Dartmouth, where I'm pursuing a double major in government and anthropology. I arrived in Hanover by way of Columbia, Missouri, where I was born and raised. I was a founding student of Columbia Independent School and one of four in the school's first graduating class. I am currently a contributor for The Dartmouth Review and am also active in Ivy Council and the Mock Trial Society. Other extracurricular interests including club rugby and the alto saxophone.

Big thanks go to Emily; to Mom, Dad, and Grant; to Sanders but not to Suhler. Thanks to the all folks at CollegeProwler for making this dream possible and to you the reader for making it a success. For those involved in the college search, good luck, and I hope you enjoy what was one of the most exciting times of my life. Please direct any and all feedback to scottgla be@collegeprowler.com

Scott Glabe

ABOUT THE EDITOR

I remember the college search process as an extremely exciting time, and it's great to be able to help out future generations of (hopefully Dartmouth) students.

I graduated last year and recieved a degree in History. Born and raised in New York City, I came to Dartmouth on a whim, but have loved my four years here. I'm serving my second term as Student Body President, am a staff writer for the Free Press, and a member of Chi Gamma Epsilon fraternity.

Best of luck to everyone – while I hope you find the best college for you, no matter where you end up the next four years are going to be incredible.

Janos Marton

Notes

....

....

....

....

....

....

....

....

....

....

....

....

....

Notes

....

....

....

....

....

....

....

....

....

....

....

....

....

Notes

....

....

....

....

....

....

....

....

....

....

....

....

Notes

....

....

....

....

....

....

....

....

....

....

....

....

....

Notes

Notes

....
....
....
....
....
....
....
....
....
....
....
....
....
....

Notes

Notes

....

....

....

....

....

....

....

....

....

....

....

....

Notes

....

....

....

....

....

....

....

....

....

....

....

....

Need More Help?

Do you have more questions about this school? Can't find a certain statistic? College Prowler is here to help. We are the best source of college information on the planet. We have a network of thousands of students who can get the latest information on any school to you ASAP. E-mail us at *info@collegeprowler.com* with your college-related questions. It's like having an older sibling show you the ropes!

Email Us Your College-Related Questions!

Check out **www.collegeprowler.com** for more details.
1.800.290.2682

Notes

....

....

....

....

....

....

....

....

....

....

....

....

....

Tell Us What Life Is Really Like At Your School!

Have you ever wanted to let people know what your school is really like? Now's your chance to help millions of high school students choose the right school.

Let your voice be heard and win cash and prizes!

Check out **www.collegeprowler.com** for more info!

Notes

....

....

....

....

....

....

....

....

....

....

....

....

....

Do You Have What It Takes To Get Admitted?

The College Prowler Road to College Counseling Program is here. An admissions officer will review your candidacy at the school of your choice and create a 12+ page personal admission plan. We rate your credentials with the same criteria used by school admissions committees. We assess your strengths and weaknesses and create a plan of action that makes a difference.

Check out **www.collegeprowler.com** or call 1.800.290.2682 for complete details.

Notes

....

....

....

....

....

....

....

....

....

....

....

....

....

Pros and Cons

Still can't figure out if this is the right school for you?
You've already read through this in-depth guide; why not
list the pros and cons? It will really help with narrowing down
your decision and determining whether or not
this school is right for you.

Pros	Cons

Notes

....

....

....

....

....

....

....

....

....

....

....

....

....

Need Help Paying For School?

Apply for our Scholarship!

College Prowler awards thousands of dollars a year
to students who compose the best essays.
E-mail *scholarship@collegeprowler.com* for more
information, or call 1.800.290.2682.

Apply now at **www.collegeprowler.com**

Notes

....

....

....

....

....

....

....

....

....

....

....

....

....

Get Paid To Rep Your City!

Make money for college!

Earn cash by telling your friends about College Prowler!

Excellent Pay + Incentives + Bonuses

Compete with reps across the nation for cash bonuses

Gain marketing and communication skills

Build your resume and gain work experience for future career opportunities

Flexible work hours; make your own schedule

Opportunities for advancement

Contact *sales@collegeprowler.com*
Apply now at **www.collegeprowler.com**

Notes

....

....

....

....

....

....

....

....

....

....

....

....

....

Do You Own A Website?

Would you like to be an affiliate of one of the fastest-growing companies in the publishing industry? Our web affiliates generate a significant income based on customers whom they refer to our website. Start making some cash now! Contact *sales@collegeprowler.com* for more information or call 1.800.290.2682

Apply now at **www.collegeprowler.com**

Notes

....

....

....

....

....

....

....

....

....

....

....

....

Reach A Market Of Over 24 Million People.

Advertising with College Prowler will provide you with an environment in which your message will be read and respected. Place your message in a College Prowler guidebook, and let us start bringing long-lasting customers to you. We deliver high-quality ads in color or black-and-white throughout our guidebooks.

Contact Joey Rahimi
joey@collegeprowler.com
412.697.1391
1.800.290.2682

Check out **www.collegeprowler.com** for more info.

Notes

....

....

....

....

....

....

....

....

....

....

....

....

....

Write For Us!
Get Published! Voice Your Opinion.

Writing a College Prowler guidebook is both fun and rewarding; our open-ended format allows your own creativity free reign. Our writers have been featured in national newspapers and have seen their names in bookstores across the country. Now is your chance to break into the publishing industry with one of the country's fastest-growing publishers!

Apply now at **www.collegeprowler.com**

Contact *editor@collegeprowler.com* or call 1.800.290.2682 for more details.

Notes

....

....

....

....

....

....

....

....

....

....

....

....

....